THE CAMPAIGN OF THE ARMY OF THE NORTH 1870–71

Louis Faidherbe

Translated by Suart Sutherland

Helion & Company Ltd

Helion & Company Limited
26 Willow Road
Solihull
West Midlands
B91 1UE
England
Tel. 0121 705 3393
Fax 0121 711 4075
Email: info@helion.co.uk
Website: www.helion.co.uk

Published by Helion & Company 2010, in association with Iser Publications

Designed and typeset by Farr out Publications, Wokingham, Berkshire
Cover designed by Farr out Publications, Wokingham, Berkshire
Printed by Lightning Source

This English translation © Stuart Sutherland 2001
Original edition: *Campagne de l'Armée du Nord en 1870-71* by Louis Faidherbe, published Paris 1872.

ISBN 978-1-906033-67-5

British Library Cataloguing-in-Publication Data.
A catalogue record for this book is available from the British Library.

All rights reserved. No part of this publication may be reproduced, stored in a retrieval system,or transmitted, in any form, or by any means, electronic, mechanical, photocopying, recording or otherwise, without the express written consent of Helion & Company Limited.

For details of other military history titles published by Helion & Company Limited contact the above address, or visit our website: http://www.helion.co.uk.

We always welcome receiving book proposals from prospective authors.

THE CAMPAIGN OF THE ARMY OF THE NORTH 1870–71

Louis Faidherbe

Translated by Suart Sutherland

General Faidherbe, painting by Rignot-Dubaux

Contents

Introduction	7
The creation of the Army of the North	9
M. Testelin is named commissary of the national defence in the region of Nord	9
Colonel Farre of the engineers is assistant to the commissary of the national defence	11
General Bourbaki is appointed commander of the Army of the North, 19 November 1870	11
Battle of Amiens or Villers-Bretonneux, 26-27 November 1870	12
The Prussian attack on and capture of the citadel of Amiens, 29 and 30 November 1870	17
Results of the battle and the capture of Amiens	19
Lieutenant General Faidherbe takes command of the Army of the North and the 3rd Military Division, 8 December 1870	19
The French recapture Ham, 10 December 1870	20
Action of Querrieux, 20 December 1870	22
Battle of Pont-Noyelles, 22 December 1870	23
Action of Achiet-le-Grand, 2 January 1871	25
Action of Béhagnies, 2 January 1871	26
Battle of Bapaume, 3 January 1871	26
Bombardment and capitulation of Péronne, 18 December 1870 to 10 January 1871	28
Reflections on the capitulation of Péronne	30
Action of Vermand, 18 January 1871	32
Battle of Saint-Quentin, 19 January 1871	33
Disbandment of the Army of the North, 7 March 1871	37

Appendices

A	The remount service of the Army of the North	38
B	The operations of the intendancy	38
C	The transport service of the Army of the North	40
D	Surrender of the citadel of Amiens	41
E	Order of the day from General Faidherbe on taking his command	41
F	Election of the officers of the *Mobiles*	42
G	Appointment of the officers of the Army of the North by virtue of the powers granted to the commanding general	42
H	Report of General von Goeben on the battle of Bapaume	43
I	Surrender of Péronne	43
J	Recapture of Saint-Quentin, 15 January 1871	44
K	History of a battery of *Mobiles*	45
L	The new shells of General de Beaulieu	46
M	The medical service of the Army of the North	47
N	Order of the day from the commanding general after the battle of Saint-Quentin	48

vi THE CAMPAIGN OF THE ARMY OF THE NORTH 1870–71

O	Examples of orders of the day of the Prussian army	48
P	Report of General Faidherbe on the impossibility of continuing the war in the Nord, at the armistice	59
Q	Order of the day to the 22nd Army Corps during the armistice	60
R	Extracts from a letter of M. Gambetta to M. Jules Favre about the inactivity of the Army of Paris	61
S	Losses of the 1st Prussian Army	64
T	Order of battle of The Army of the North about mid-January 1871	64

Introduction

The author of this work, Louis (Léon-César) Faidherbe, was born in 1818 in Lille, in the north of France, to a lower-middle-class family. He entered the prestigious Engineering School at Metz in 1840, and on graduation was sent to Algeria in 1843 as a lieutenant of engineers, and then to the West Indian island of Guadeloupe in 1848. After service once more in Algeria, for which he was awarded the Legion of Honour, Faidherbe was posted to the French west African colony of Senegal in 1851 as commander of engineers and second-in-command. In 1854 he was promoted major and named governor. Faidherbe remained in Senegal until 1865, and during his period as governor he tried to improve the material and moral lot of the inhabitants. There was some fighting with tribes in the interior, and in 1858 were raised the first native troops in French service, the *Tirailleurs sénégalais*, who would later become famous. Faidherbe also attempted to foster education, commerce and the towns, although claims that he was very successful as governor have been challenged. Nonetheless, he retained an abiding interest in Senegal for the remainder of his life.

Upon leaving Senegal, Faidherbe went to Algeria, where when the Franco-Prussian War broke out in July 1870 he was serving as commandant of the Constantine Military Division with the rank of lieutenant general. Faidherbe's pronounced republicanism and intellectualism (he was the author of not a few books on customs and language in west Africa) made him doubly distasteful to the army of Napoleon III and is reflected in his complete absence from the numerous wars and actions which the French army took part during the 1850s and 1860s. However, once Napoleon's regime fell on 4 September 1870 after the disaster of Sedan, Faidherbe was recalled to France and on 18 November given command of the so-called Army of the North, a formation which was being raised in what was known as the region of the North. This land, which encompassed the departments of Pas-du-Calais, Nord and Somme, was the premier industrial zone of France. Dotted with fortresses of greater or lesser strength, it was extremely rich and well populated and thus offered great resources on which the new French government could draw. The line of fortresses offered a secure last redoubt against German advances, and free communications to Britain and Belgium allowed supplies to arrive from those nations.

As a native of the region and a staunch republican, Faidherbe was a natural choice as commander, despite his lack of combat experience. Moreover, he was a modest man, almost painfully honest and well aware that the raw material with which he had to fashion his army was most inadequate. Nonetheless, by the end of 1870 Faidherbe had made fairly good progress, although not to the extent he wished when government pressure to link up with the army in Paris increased by the end of November. However, he dutifully moved south and engineered a striking success by capturing the fortress of Ham, thereby cutting German rail communications to the west and threatening their rear areas. The German reaction was belated, but on 23 December Faidherbe was able to fight a partly successful delaying action east of Amiens on what would become the World War I battlefield of Villers-Bretonneux. However, he realized his troops were fast deteriorating in the wintry weather and that German reinforcements were coming in, and so he withdrew north to Arras.

His next task was set as the relief of the important fortress of Péronne, then besieged by the Germans, and in a series of closely contested fights around Bapaume on 3 January 1871 the French made some progress. However, Faidherbe did not feel his troops up to further effort and withdrew northwest; perhaps not the best decision under the circumstances, for the Germans too were weak and were preparing to lift the siege of Péronne, but it was a consistent one for Faidherbe. In fact, Péronne capitulated on the 9th. Once more the government urged on him the necessity of doing something to divert the German efforts at Paris, and Faidherbe determined on a move southeast to cut across German communications. The movement was unfortunately not the easiest, and it was made more difficult in that the French army was marching across the front of the German forces, who could readily observe and harass it. Moreover, the terrible winter weather and the poor condition of Faidherbe's troops complicated the manoeuvre, and by the time Faidherbe's army arrived around Saint-Quentin the Germans had anticipated it. All that the French could do on 19 January was to fight another defensive battle in and around the town against attacks from the south and west. Faidherbe's men fought well in parts, but their morale was low, and in spite of their numerical superiority they were forced into a disorderly retreat, shedding refugees with every mile, until once more they were under the shelter of the fortresses. There they remained until the war ended.

Faidherbe was not subject to as scathing criticism as other republican generals for his conduct of the campaign, chiefly because he was intelligent enough to appreciate the limitations of his men and also because the government did not attach as much importance to the northern front as it did to those of the Loire and southeast. Nonetheless, he effectively left active service in 1871, but his conduct of the northern campaign was widely applauded, and he was elected a deputy, and then a senator of France. He continued to publish and be interested in African affairs until his death in 1889 in Paris.

In the wake of the Franco-German War there appeared a host of volumes by participants, those on the French side naturally taking pains to emphasize their role or de-emphasize their part in the disasters as the case was. Faidherbe contributed to this deluge by having published in Paris in 1872 a slim volume entitled *Campagne de l'Armée du Nord* (*Campaign of the Army of the North*). It sets out in some detail the operations of the Army of the North and includes many appendices which give supporting evidence and documents. Certain of Faidherbe's opinions were not shared by his principal later German opponent, General August von Goeben, and Goeben, himself a writer and thinker of some stature, replied in a volume that year to refute Faidherbe's claims. Faidherbe riposted with *Army of the North: a response to General Goeben* in 1873, and the controversy continued until Goeben died in 1880.

The work translated here is the 1872 volume. It has been reproduced in its entirety, and the presentation of the original has largely been followed. Some restructuring of paragraphs has occurred, but the wording has not been affected. Modern-day place names have been substituted and supplementary information added. An appendix with a detailed order of battle for the Army of the North about the middle of January 1871 has been taken from Pierre Lehautcourt [B.-E. Palat], *Histoire de la guerre de 1870-71* (15 volumes, Paris and Nancy, 1901-8).

Stuart Sutherland

The Campaign of the Army of the North 1870–71

The creation of the Army of the North

The Army of the North had never more than 50,000 combatants, this figure including two detached brigades, one in the east and one at Abbeville. It was not, therefore, in point of size of the same importance as the republic's other armies. But it was notable for its fine organization, its discipline and the excellent spirit which continuously animated it. In the actions it fought it contributed in no small manner to re-establishing and maintaining the honour of the flag, which had been so deeply affected by the unprecedented disasters and capitulations which had thrown the country into a hopeless situation. The history of the army therefore deserves some attention, and this account will present the most basic information about its organization and operations.

M. Testelin is named commissary of the national defence in the region of Nord

When M. Gambetta, the minister of the interior, devoting himself entirely to the defence of the country, left Paris in a balloon, he bestowed the fullest powers on men in the regions who because of their patriotism and energy seemed the most proper to appoint for the defence of the departments. In the north this man was M. A. Testelin. Appointed government commissioner for the departments of the Aisne, Nord, Pas-du-Calais and Somme, he was to employ the considerable military resources of this rich country. He therefore asked the generals who succeeded to the command of the 3rd Military Division, which encompassed this region, to take measures to that effect, giving them all the authority with which he had been invested and all the means of action they could wish. He urged them to organize forces which could go through a campaign or which could at least prevent the raids of small detachments fleecing the country, and which were far away from the as yet distant enemy forces.

All his efforts were in vain; he could achieve nothing. Only fortresses could be defended, he was told. And at the same time the improvement of the elements of the defence, which had been disorganized by the despatch of materials to Paris, was not sought. It sufficed to clothe and arm the *Gardes Mobiles*, without any concern about forming the proper staffs. As to the regulars, they had been drawn from seven or eight regional depots, and detachments from them had been despatched to the centre of the country to be absorbed into other units. Each depot had more than 1,000 men, with incomplete staffs of two companies. By way of artillery there was but one battery at Lille, and that incapable of service. Last, for cavalry the depot of the 7th Dragoons could with difficulty supply several troopers as escorts.

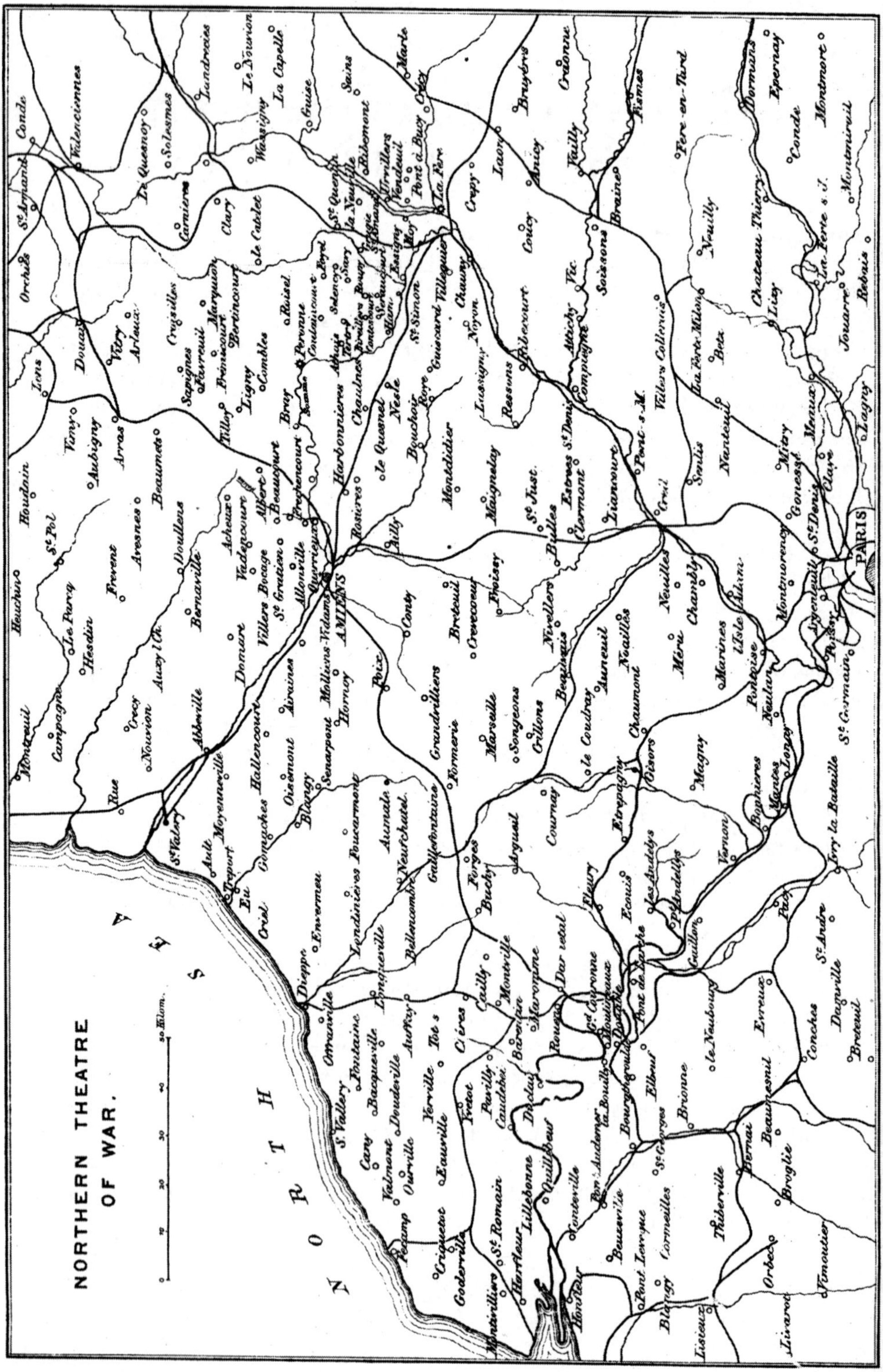

Colonel Farre of the engineers is assistant to the commissary of the national defence

In order to end this situation, about 15 October M. Testelin went to see Colonel Farre, director of the works at Lille, and made him a member of the commission for national defence with the rank of major general. Work commenced at once. The available elements were collected, former soldiers found from whom staffs could be established, an inventory was made of all material in the fortresses so as to understand their resources and more efficiently divide them; last, material was found for the immediate creation of provisional batteries. The zeal of the officials charged with this task was stimulated by all means possible. This tiresome task, which could not be accomplished without surmounting all sorts of difficulties, and in the face of a military divisional staff which was at least indifferent, had begun to show results when on 22 October General Bourbaki took command of the region of the north.

General Bourbaki is appointed commander of the Army of the North, 19 November 1870

Although deeply discouraged by our reverses, General Bourbaki was not indifferent to the attempts at organization which had been started. He supported them with all his power and took General Farre as his chief of staff for the army corps of the North he wished to raise. But it must be said that his faith in the efficacy of a prolongation of the defence failed him. He, who had just seen the destruction of magnificent armies, could not pin much hope on a collection of recruits, escaped prisoners and badly armed and very inexperienced militiamen. Moreover, public opinion was unfavourable to him. He was distrusted because of his former intimacy with the court, his command of the Imperial Guard, which he had led at the start of the war, and above all because of his mysterious, fantastic voyage from Metz to London.

The troops available were line infantry and *Gardes Mobiles*. The infantry had fairly numerous forces in the depots, without staffs. As for the latter, it was battalions with an effective strength of 1,200 to 1,500 men, and which as a result were too large to be handled effectively. It was ordered that the battalions which would make up the field army have five companies of 150 men and three officers. Two new batteries were raising and others were being created, especially of 12-pounders. From the fortress of La Fère came all the materials there which were not needed for its defence, and which provided valuable support. The transport of this material to Douai was finished the evening of the same day La Fère was invested. General Treuille de Beaulieu and the director, Colonel Brian, imparted the greatest activity to the works of the artillery direction at Douai, which had to supply the fortresses without forgetting the requirements of the campaign and the supply of cartridges, etc.

From the minister of the navy were obtained 50 large-calibre cannon to reinforce the armament of the fortresses. There was feverish activity everywhere, and on 6 November at least the provisional regiments of the first division of the 22nd Corps could be established.

The question of the staffs was full of difficulties, but it was resolved by the surrenders of Sedan and Metz. These disastrous events brought to the north a fairly large number of escaping officers and non-commissioned officers, all energetic and full of keenness. Sadly, not all of them were kept at Lille, but there were enough to form the major parts of the staffs of the 1st Division. More came later, and they allowed new formations to be established.

Each brigade consisted of seven battalions, one of *chasseurs à pied*, a provisional regiment of three battalions and a provisional regiment of the *Garde Mobile* of three battalions. The combined strength was 5,500 men. Lieutenant Colonel Lecointe, a distinguished officer who had escaped from Metz, received command of the first brigade, and a distinguished veteran of the engineers, Lieutenant Colonel Rittier, who had reentered service, was designated as commander of the second brigade.

The artillery, placed under Commandant Charon, an escapee from Sedan, and whose activity contributed greatly to the organization of the army's artillery, did not have more than three batteries of 4-pounders and one of 12-pounders, then forming. The raising of two new 12-pounder batteries was ordered, their crews sailors taken from the *fusiliers marins* who had just arrived in the north. These 12-pounders were pulled across all sorts of ground by the magnificent Flemish horses which the district had in abundance.

As far as cavalry was concerned, there were four small depots of dragoons in the northern fortresses. They were assembled at Lille and a single depot of the *Dragons du Nord* was created under Captain de Cabannes, promoted major, for the organization of this corps, which after a ministerial order became the 7th Dragoons. Horses were bought (Appendix A), troopers collected here and there, and soon two squadrons had been formed. Moreover, two squadrons were raised from the police of the region and swiftly made ready to march.

The question of clothing and equipment was extremely hard to resolve (Appendix B). Often people were obliged to be content with a little less in order to expedite matters. Moreover, more than once the readying of the troops for service was delayed because of difficulties of this sort, which were removed thanks to the energetic aid of M. Richard, the army's chief intendant.

On 19 November the 1st Division was ready to march, and the formation of the corps had begun with the establishment of a 2nd Division, when General Bourbaki, following hostile demonstrations by the inhabitants, gave up the command of 22nd Corps by ministerial order and for the moment turned it over to General Farre.

Lieutenant Colonel Loysel and the other staff officers followed General Bourbaki, and everything would have been brought to a stop if General Farre, who had been left all alone, had not found in Lieutenant Colonel de Villenoisy of the engineers, who had escaped from Metz, and in several other engineer officers, who took up the duties of staff officers, a total devotion to their work and remarkable capacities. The task was carried on without cease and with the help of Colonel Lecointe, now promoted general. While the administrative services were organized and placed on the best footing possible by the care of the chief intendant, requisitions were made by the civilian authorities so as to organize the bare minimum of a provisions convoy and to horse the wagons of the engineer park. Major transactions were made for clothing and equipment in such a way to largely furnish the needs of the units and the expenditures of a campaign.

Battle of Amiens or Villers-Bretonneux, 26-27 November 1870

Things were therefore about ready to set in motion when Amiens was threatened by the strong forces of the 1st German Army under General Manteuffel. The Bordeaux government believed this important town could not be captured without an attempt to defend it. In consequence, a third brigade was formed with all speed, and on the 24th the unit concentrated. The 1st Division had the 1st Brigade under General Lecointe and the 2nd under Colonel Derroja, the 2nd Division the 1st Brigade under Colonel du Bessol. The 2nd Brigade of the 2nd Division was forming under Colonel Rittier. It sent a chasseur battalion and two other just organized battalions to guard the Somme crossings between Péronne and Corbie.

There were also two squadrons of dragoons, two squadrons of police and six batteries (four of 4-, two of 12-pounders). A seventh, 12-pounder, battery, was not ready until the last minute. Arriving at 10 a.m. by railway from Amiens, it fought gloriously [at the battle of Villers-Bretonneux] until 1 p.m. Last, a engineer company with a small park completed this small army, which had a total size of 17,500 men. When joined by the 8,000-man garrison of Amiens under General Paulze d'Ivoy, there were about 25,000 combatants.

Before he left, General Bourbaki planned to establish 22nd Corps, as soon as it had been formed, south of Amiens along the railway line to Rouen. This position was a very good one from which to move on Beauvais and Creil, but not if the enemy advanced in force to the Somme by the roads from Montdidier and Roye and along the railway from Tergnier. An attack from this direction had to be repulsed. So as to avoid camping out, which was too unpleasant at the time of year, the three brigades were billeted in Amiens and the villages to its east as far as Corbie and Villers-Bretonneux. During all the campaign the Army of the North was billeted, which was possible in the prosperous lands of Picardy, Artois and Flanders, where large villages are so plentiful.

Because it was important to keep a good hold on the line of the Somme between Péronne and Corbie, so as to protect the line of retreat and the Northern Railway Line, three battalions were sent to this river from Lille and Arras. Its bridges were destroyed, except for those our troops held. But the position could not be limited to the right bank of the Somme, which was very strong because of the heights which dominate this river's swampy valley. Our small army would have been immobilized in this totally defensive position and the defence of Amiens would have been reduced to the entrenchments built around the town by the local authorities. Moreover, although these entrenchments were in good positions they were incomplete; their profiles were low, their extent enormous. In order to hold this ground with a chance of success and fight the greatly superior enemy artillery, the 12 imperfectly equipped guns which the town had managed to place there would have had to have been reinforced by the 42 guns of 22nd Corps, but this arrangement would have compromised Corbie, the key to the Amiens-Arras railway. As a result, General Farre decided to post himself on the heights along the left bank of the Somme between the Somme and the Avre, their highest point at the small village of Villers-Bretonneux and whose crest was covered by the woods of Blagny[-Tronville] and Cachy. There, where the two brigades billetted outside Amiens could be rapidly assembled, they could resist the main body of the enemy, which had been reported to be to the east. The line ran at right angles from Villiers[-aux-Erables] to Cachy and Gentelles, its right adjoining the valley of the Avre. A second line of defence, taking Villiers-Bretonneux as the pivot for the two lines, followed the ridge which falling from there to Longueau, and which was covered in woods and flanked the approaches to Amiens. A retreat towards the right bank of the Somme could be done using gentle slopes falling towards the river and the numerous bridges retained along this part of its length. The position was quite good, but it was too long for our troops and could not be shortened. Moreover, the enemy did not give us time to add some entrenchments before Villers-Bretonneux, the key to the position, and at the village of Boves, which covered the gap at Longueau where the Avre joins the Somme.

The 3rd Brigade, commanded by Colonel du Bessol, occupied Corbie and the surrounding villages, Villers-Bretonneux, Cachy and Gentelles. The 2nd, under the command of General Derroja, was placed at Boves, on the Avre, at Camon, on the Somme, and in the neighbouring ground. The 1st Brigade was at Amiens under General Lecointe.

The troops had not been fully assembled on the ground when on the evening of the 23rd a company of *francs-tireurs* engaged the enemy at Villiers-aux-Érables, reporting fairly strong forces there. Next day an offensive reconnaissance was sent there by Colonel du Bessol. An outstanding fight took place near Mézières[-en-Santerre]. The enemy, repulsed at the point of the bayonet and ejected from the woods, did not stop until Bouchoir, carrying off eight wagons of dead and wounded. Our losses were inconsiderable; sadly, however, Lieutenant Laviolette of the artillery was mortally wounded by a bullet in the chest.

On the 25th the terrain was scoured by lancers, whom our advanced posts fired on at a distance. But the afternoon of the next day a fairly stiff fight occurred at Gentelles, where was posted a part of the 20th Chasseur Battalion, supported by a company of the 43rd Provisional Regiment, drawn from Villers-Bretonneux. A Prussian column from Moreuil entered the valley of the Avre at the villages of Fouencamps and Boves. The first place, weakly occupied as a guard post, was evacuated, but the enemy was then halted by the skirmishers of the 1st Chasseur Battalion and the 24th Line Infantry Regiment, who gave them heavy losses. A field officer of the first order, Commandant Jan, died a glorious death during this affair, which ended in our favour.

As the incidents of this day occurred, dispositions were made to reinforce the threatened points. At an early hour the 1st Brigade was ordered to post itself between the 3rd and 2nd brigades. All the 3rd Brigade was placed in Villers-Bretonneux and the positions of Cachy and Gentelles were also reinforced. These movements were ordered to end when night fell.

The 1st and 2nd brigades were ordered to send two battalions to reconnoitre along the line of heights between Villers-Bretonneux and Longueau the following day so as to adequately scout the ground and to have their other units ready to march to the aid of the positions attacked. The weather was rainy and the ground hardly passable because of its state. The enemy's efforts had not been considerable enough on the 26th that a general action could not be assumed to take place the following day.

But the weather cleared up during the night; reports which arrived during the morning of the 27th were dangerous. It was agreed that General Paulze d'Ivoy would post himself with all the garrison before the entrenchments in order to protect Amiens. He was given a 12-pounder battery manned by sailors, which had just left a train arriving from Douai. The enemy soon showed themselves in force, and a lively action began at Boves and Gentelles.

General Lecointe passed through the Gentelles wood with part of the 1st Brigade, drive back the enemy, relieved Gentelles in a close-fought action, and continued to advance until night without meeting serious resistance until the wood of Domart[-sur-la-Luce], which was taken in a brilliant fashion by the 4th Battalion of Nord [*Gardes Mobiles*]. After arriving near the village of this name, General Lecointe decided to fall back on Longueau, since he had no news of the rest of the action and was very far from Amiens. At 8 p.m. he learned the outcome of the battle.

Part of the village of Cachy was taken by the Prussians despite the heroic resistance of the battalion of the 43rd assigned its defence, and it had to evacuate this position after it was very strongly attacked. Its commander had been killed and seven officers put out of action. The commanding general resumed the offensive by the skirmish line bordering the Villers wood, the 20th Chasseur Battalion and the 9th Battalion of *Mobiles*. These troops advanced at a run and briskly retook the village.

Three reserve battalions on the skirts of the wood were advanced to hold more firmly the visibly weakening long gap between Cachy and Villers. At this time, 2:30 p.m., the fight had assumed the greatest possible intensity at Villers, where Colonel du Bessol had just been wounded after having had a horse killed under him. All our reserves were engaged, and some of our soldiers lost the ground on the south side of the railway cutting. Nothing was spared to redress the balance here, and the 12-pounder battery and an 8-pounder battery were posted well in front, left of the village. From there the *infanterie de marine*, the 2nd Chasseurs and the engineer company drove the enemy back for a great way. But to the right of Villers, despite all our efforts, the *Gardes Mobiles* were finally forced to yield, which had a bad effect on the morale of the regulars fighting with them. The two 4-pounder batteries, advanced to the right of the village, had used up their ammunition in supporting the skirmishers and replying to more than 40 enemy cannon, which our four batteries held in check all day. At last, with ammunition gone (there was then a great lack of this in the north), the long line from Villers-Bretonneux to Cachy having been bent and a Prussian battery which had established itself close to the latter place having taken our troops in flank, General Farre ordered a retreat. He ordered Lieutenant Colonel de Villenoisy to fall back along the Amiens road with part of the troops, the remainder being directed to Corbie, with the major part of the artillery, escorted by the 2nd Chasseurs, the *infanterie de marine* and the engineers. These last had always been victorious and had advanced very far, and they entered Villers at the same time as the enemy. Several detachments of the *infanterie de marine* defended the village streets with the proven valour of this corps. At this time we suffered the most serious losses. The engineer company was surrounded, and it was not until night that its two captains and the great majority of its men could rejoin.

On the right was the weakest part of the corps, and it could do no more than have small posts at Boves, Cagny and Longueau, which had to count principally on the protection of the works raised by the garrison of Amiens in front of the town. General Paulze d'Ivoy had occupied the works with his troops during the morning, and he send forward from the village of Dury a reconnaissance force consisting of the 2nd Chasseurs, the 43rd Line Infantry Regiment and the 4th Battalion of the Somme *Gardes Mobiles*. This detachment advanced quite far, but it was not strong and had no artillery. It was forced to retreat on encountering a superior enemy force and retook post behind the works, where there were nine unequipped cannon.

It was hard to halt the rush of the enemy at this place until the arrival of a 12-pounder rifled battery, manned by sailors from Brest and commanded by Lieutenant Meunier. These courageous gunners responded energetically to the Prussian fire, not without suffering losses, the most regrettable of which was that of their heroic commander, who was cut in two by a shell after having been wounded three times. The battery had been totally dismounted when it was aided by a company of sailors, commanded by Lieutenants

Rolland and Bertrand, which came with 4-pounders loaned from the *Garde Nationale*, and they continued the battle until nightfall.

The evident inferiority of our artillery and our troops' retreat behind the entrenchments allowed the Prussians to establish themselves in the half-burned village of Dury and that of Saint-Fuscien, which they bypassed, in such a manner that the position of Boves was outflanked early on. The ruins of the old chateau of Boves were held by two companies, one from the 33rd Line Regiment, the other from the 24th. Colonel Pittié, with the 2nd Battalion 24th and the 4th Battalion of the *Mobiles* of Nord, reconnoitred the right bank of the Avre valley, while a battalion of the 33rd and part of the 5th Battalion of the *Mobiles* of Nord advanced towards Saint-Fuscien, which was still thought to be in our hands. The 1st Battalion 24th was held in reserve at the railway station of Longueau. All these troops were attacked in a very lively fashion. The energetic resistance of the companies entrenched in the ruins of Boves prevented a direct enemy advance and forced the latter to cross through the swamps, covered by the wood of Cottenchy. As a result there was a pause, during which the left-wing battalions continued to advance and took part in the capture of Gentelles. But soon the battalions on the right wing, 1st Chasseurs, 33rd Line and 5th *Mobiles*, were outflanked through the swamp and taken in their rear by the Prussians, who were now masters of Saint-Fuschien and Cagny, and they were pushed back on Longueau. Colonel Derroja rallied the troops and charged with the bayonet. This charge, led in a vigorous fashion by Commandant Zédé of the 33rd and a captain of the 5th Battalion of *Mobiles* (who was badly wounded, and it is to be regretted that his name cannot be mentioned), halted the enemy pursuit. The late hour put an end to the fight, and the rest of the evening was used in rallying the troops at Longueau.

Without prejudging the definitive decision which could have been taken, it was ordered that the troops be assembled in the streets of Amiens after several hours of rest. There they were issued with two days' rations and all that was available in cartridges, and they were also made ready for a retreat or for a defence of the citadel. Colonel du Bessol approved these dispositions. Only General Paulze d'Ivoy spoke of resistance in the entrenchments around the town, but for that he needed cannon, which could not be provided because nearly all their ammunition had been expended. These opinions were telegraphed to the commanding general, who after mature thought gave at 3 a.m. the order for a general retreat of the Army of the North.

The movement began around 5:30 a.m., at Amiens and Corbie, in four columns. The first, under General Lecointe, went towards Doullens; the second, led by General Paulze d'Ivoy, took the Pas[-en-Artois] road. General Farre went due north with the third column, the fourth taking the road along the railway line to Albert and Achiet.

The regulars kept complete order, but part of the *Gardes Mobiles*, and, it must be admitted, some of their officers, left for home. At Amiens an unfortunate event disturbed the order of the tails of the first two columns. Some *Gardes Nationales* fired off their arms before breaking them; these shots caused disorder among the troops, who were being issued cartridges. It was thought there was an attack, and the squadron of police which was to have been the rearguard galloped off and cut the column in two. This regrettable incident caused the loss of a line of empty wagons and a certain amount of cartridges, which were soaked, a necessary step since some of the enemy were armed with Chassepot rifles. Nonetheless, Colonel Crouzat of the auxiliary army, commander of the *Garde Nationale* artillery, succeeded in bringing off to Abbeville and Montreuil the majority of the cannon belonging to the town and department. Amiens was evacuated practically without loss; a garrison was left in the citadel.

The Prussian attack on and capture of the citadel of Amiens, 29 and 30 November 1870

The citadel, abandoned at the beginning of September, had been reoccupied in the first days of October when a strong Prussian advance on Amiens was thought likely. The fort was to protect the town to the north, earthworks defending it at other points. Twenty-two smoothbore cannon (8-, 12-, 16-pounders, howitzers and mortars) were placed on the ramparts so as to cover the glacis and sweep the ditches, but the commander of the *Garde Mobile* artillery did not think it necessary to make provision for a defence against the town. The 1st battery of the *Gardes Mobiles* of the Somme, which had been told off to work these guns, arrived at its post on 27 November, while the guns were sounding in the simultaneous fights at Boves and Dury.

At 3 a.m. the two depot companies of the 43rd, which the previous day had received an order to rejoin their battalion at Dury during the night, left the citadel to retreat towards Arras, and as so there were no more than 130 artillerymen left in the citadel. At the same time the commander of the *Mobile* artillery, M. Vœrhaye, having gone to the prefecture, was told that the French army was to retreat. Since the prefect had no instructions for him, he went to General Paulze d'Ivoy, who gave him the 1st, 2nd and 7th companies of the 10th Battalion of the *Garde Mobile* of Nord in order to garrison the fortress.

As soon as this reinforcement arrived, which brought the strength of the garrison to about 450 men, the commander of the citadel, Captain Vogel, raised the drawbridge and posted sentries on the ramparts. Until 9 p.m. the garrison helped the retreat of the French army, which fell back along the Doullens road. The morning of the 28th was taken up with installing. Towards 10, the members of the municipal council went to the commander to learn his intentions. In response to their request, Commandant Vogel promised to remain on the defensive in order to spare the town, his full provisions allowing him to submit to a long siege.

At noon, two detachments of several hundred men advanced towards the citadel, and two trumpeters rode forward to demand the entry of negotiators. Commandant Vogel had the drawbridge lowered and met the Prussian officers. Called on to surrender, he replied that even under the favourable conditions which were promised the citadel would not surrender, but that he would not take the initiative in acts of war. The Prussians thereupon retired, leaving several guard posts in the town, and the day was marked by nothing more than comings and goings around the fort and the desertion of 15 *Mobiles*, who by arrangement with their non-commissioned officer had abandoned the advance post in front of the citadel during the night.

At the end of the day, a new parliamentary presented himself, bearing a letter in which General von Goeben, rendering homage to the courage and patriotic sentiments of the commandant, said that he had been abandoned by the French army and that there was no point in continuing an impossible resistance in circumstances which could not affect his honour. This letter, as clever as it was flattering, did not impress the commandant, who gave the same reply as previously.

The morning of the 29th was passed in expectation of an attack. The Prussians had used the night to pierce the walls and roofs of the houses neighbouring the ramparts.

Towards 11 a parliamentary appeared and made a third summons, and on a new refusal he announced that fire would be opened within a quarter of an hour. The commandant immediately had the assembly beaten and went rapidly and unhesitatingly to his post.

Ten minutes had barely gone by when a very strong fusillade from the houses between the church of the Saint-Pierre suburb and the garden of Plantes was directed on every part of the citadel which overlooked the town, that is on bastions Nos 1 to 5 and the curtain joining them. This fire was replied to by rifle and artillery fire, which caused the enemy numerous casualties. The action having begun, Commandant Vogel toured the ramparts to organize and direct the defence. A man of proven valour, he showed calm and boldness and gave confidence to the least courageous, for without taking account of danger he exposed himself to the shots, which in certain places fell like hail.

Finally, towards midday, he had just ended his dangerous round when he arrived at Bastion No 5, the most threatened. There he spoke to Sergeant Major Savary, ordering him to cease fire on the town since the enemy artillery was not responding. The latter explained that the bastion was so overlooked by the tax office in front of the embrasure that it was impossible to show oneself without being fired on, and that for that reason it appeared to him to be necessary to demolish it. The commandant replied that that was a different matter and went forward to examine the position of the building. But barely had he arrived at the embrasure when he was seen and was mortally wounded by a bullet which hit him in his right side and went through his body. The direction of the defence fell to the commander of the *Mobile* artillery. Told that Bastions Nos 4 and 5 were taking rifle fire from the clock tower of the Saint-Pierre church, he ordered a gun to be laid on the church. Three shells demolished the tower and ended the fire.

At 4 p.m., the enemy having fallen back, the commandant ordered sentries posted. From this time only some rifle shots were exchanged with the enemy posts. The night passed without incident, and since a night attack seemed unlikely and there were other arrangements, the troops retired to their rooms to prepare to awake early the next day. Towards midnight the doctor and the chaplain told the commandant and the unit commanders that further resistance was impossible, since the citadel's commandant had been killed and the artillerymen of the *Mobiles*, all natives of Amiens, found themselves in the disagreeable position of having to fire on their homes to defend themselves. A council of war was called and it was decided to allow the entrance of a parliamentary. The commandant therefore raised white flags on Bastions 1 and 5 and awaited the break of day.

At 7 a.m. two Prussian officers arrived. The basis for the capitulation having been presented, they asked that the commandant raise the white flag on the highest building of the citadel so that it might be seen by the enemy batteries. During the night these had been positioned on all sides for a bombardment to commence at 8. One of these officers, his eyes bandaged, entered the citadel and was conducted to the commandant to discuss the matter. After half an hour he left, his eyes rebandaged, to take the news to his commanders, since among other things it had been requested that the *Mobile* battery, which was entirely of young men of Amiens, was to be paroled. This condition was rejected; it was not even allowed the officers. The definitive clauses of the surrender were accordingly agreed to by Commandant Vœrhage and the Prussian officer (Appendix D). At 8 a.m. the parliamentary left, and with sadness the garrison learned the result of the negotiations. An hour later the enemy entered the fort.

Results of the battle and the capture of Amiens

The battle of Amiens had been very honourable for an army so rapidly improvised as the Army of the North. Its enemies expressed their astonishment on finding documents on the dead which testified they had been in service only a few weeks; they had believed that the battle had been with veterans. The artillery had conducted itself excellently; 22nd Corps had not left a single piece in enemy hands. Our losses were heavy enough. Over a six-hour battle we had had 266 killed and 1,117 wounded; moreover, a thousand were missing and many *Mobiles* had left. The enemy, who had had 35,000 men, had had larger losses in killed or wounded, according to the most moderate calculations. In Villers-Bretonneux alone, where we had left 114 killed and 500 wounded (accounted for by the ambulance), Prussian doctors counted 500 killed and 1,200 wounded. Nothing demonstrates the scale of the enemy losses more than the lack of any pursuit. Only three days later did the enemy advance along the right bank of the Somme to within a day's march, and they did not continue, Manteuffel's army going towards Normandy.

After the retreat from Amiens, the units were directed to their depots in order to reorganize, and the formation of new units was undertaken without cease. The creation of artillery was redoubled in activity. The lack of ammunition had been felt in the most unfortunate manner in the battle of Amiens. Commandant Charon, promoted lieutenant colonel, added to each existing or forming battery a half-line of caissons. Each infantry battalion was accompanied by a cartridge caisson, using the Gribeauval-pattern caissons, of which there was a large supply. In brief, there was the greatest activity everywhere to continue the struggle.

Lieutenant General Faidherbe takes command of the Army of the North and the 3rd Military Division, 8 December 1870

By a decree of 18 November 1870, General Faidherbe, commanding the Constantine division, had been called to replace General Bourbaki in the command of 22nd Corps, which formed the Army of the North (Appendix E). In the interests of the service, he had also been given command of the 3rd Military Division, which consisted of the departments of the Nord, Pas-du-Calais and Somme, as well as the neighbouring territory which had not been invaded.

22nd Corps was raised to three divisions, i.e.: 1st Division (General Lecointe): 1st Brigade, Colonel Derroja; 2nd Brigade, Lieutenant Colonel Pittié. 2nd Division (General Paulze d'Ivoy): 1st Brigade, Colonel du Bessol; 2nd Brigade Lieutenant-Colonel de Gislain. 3rd Division (Admiral Moulac): 1st Brigade, Post-Captain Payen; 2nd Brigade, Commander Lagrange.

The brigades of the two first divisions were formed according to the initial pattern. Those of the third were different: the 1st Brigade was composed of a battalion of chasseurs, a three-battalion regiment of *fusiliers marins* and a regiment of *Mobiles* (Appendix F). The 2nd Brigade was formed from *Mobiles* and *Mobilisés*. The staffs were created with the aid of officers from the army and *Mobiles*; the administrative services also received the necessary complements.

The artillery was considerably strengthened. To the seven batteries which had fought at Amiens were added four more, to the point where each division was equipped with three batteries and there were two more as a reserve. In addition, a reserve park was organized.

However, Normandy had been invaded, Rouen taken and Le Havre threatened. The ultimate goal of the Prussian army was to arrive at the sea. General Faidherbe understood that a strong diversion was necessary to save the second most important commercial port of France. Barely several days after his arrival from Algeria on 8 December, he restarted operations. At the headquarters in Lille he left Lieutenant Colonel de Villenoisy, Lieutenant Colonel Rittier and the artillery commander, Quiellé, to continue the work of organization and to send him battalions, squadrons and batteries as they were formed. As we have said, he could in this way enter into a campaign with three divisions instead of the three brigades which had fought at Amiens. These troops consisted of 30,000 combatants with 60 cannon.

The French recapture Ham, 10 December 1870

He sent the 1st Division of 22nd Corps towards Saint-Quentin, whose approach caused enemy detachments to fall back towards La Fère and Ham. General Lecointe, who commanded the division, arrived at Ham on the 9th at 6 p.m. He considered rightly that it was necessary to make a sharp assault on the chateau in order to take it in order not to leave the enemy time to reconnoitre and receive reinforcements. It was in this chateau that Prince Louis-Napoleon, later Napoleon III, had been imprisoned by King Louis-Philippe after his second attempt at a rising, at Boulogne-sur-Mer.

Three columns from a battalion, each supported by two cannon, went through the town by various routes and arrived at the esplanade of the fort. One of them detached a company towards the railway station, which was taken along with its defenders. After a summons had been rejected, several cannon shots were fired against the towers, without result. The entry was difficult to see and had been strongly barricaded. However, about 2 a.m. the defenders asked to surrender. This capitulation gave us 210 prisoners, of whom 12 were engineer officers. Arriving at Ham on the 10th with the remainder of the corps, the commanding general found on advancing to the south that the country was free from the enemy.

On the 12th and 13th he reconnoitred La Fère but could not consider a siege, having seen it could not be taken with the force he had. He decided on the 14th to move towards Amiens, sending out parties to make surprise attacks on the enemy detachments and convoys at Chauny, Roye and elsewhere.

The appearance beneath the walls of La Fère of the Army of the North gave great concern to the enemy generals, since they believed it to have been destroyed on 27 November. Orders went out for a concentration of force and VIII Corps was promptly recalled from Normandy, whose invasion had been imprudently described by several Prussian newspapers. General Faidherbe had therefore attained his goal, and he now had to prepare to fight the forces gathering against him.

The march of 22nd Corps took place in great order and without problems. The 2nd Division, under General Paulze d'Ivoy, had joined the 1st during its march. The little cavalry available, two dragoon squadrons, operated in small detachments, quickly became seasoned and made several successful long-distance raids. The Moulac Division joined the first two.

Upon approaching Amiens, it was confirmed that the movement on Le Havre had been halted, Dieppe had been evacuated and that bodies of troops were moving om Montreuil and Breteuil. General Manteuffel had abandoned, at least temporarily, his plans for the

NARRATIVE

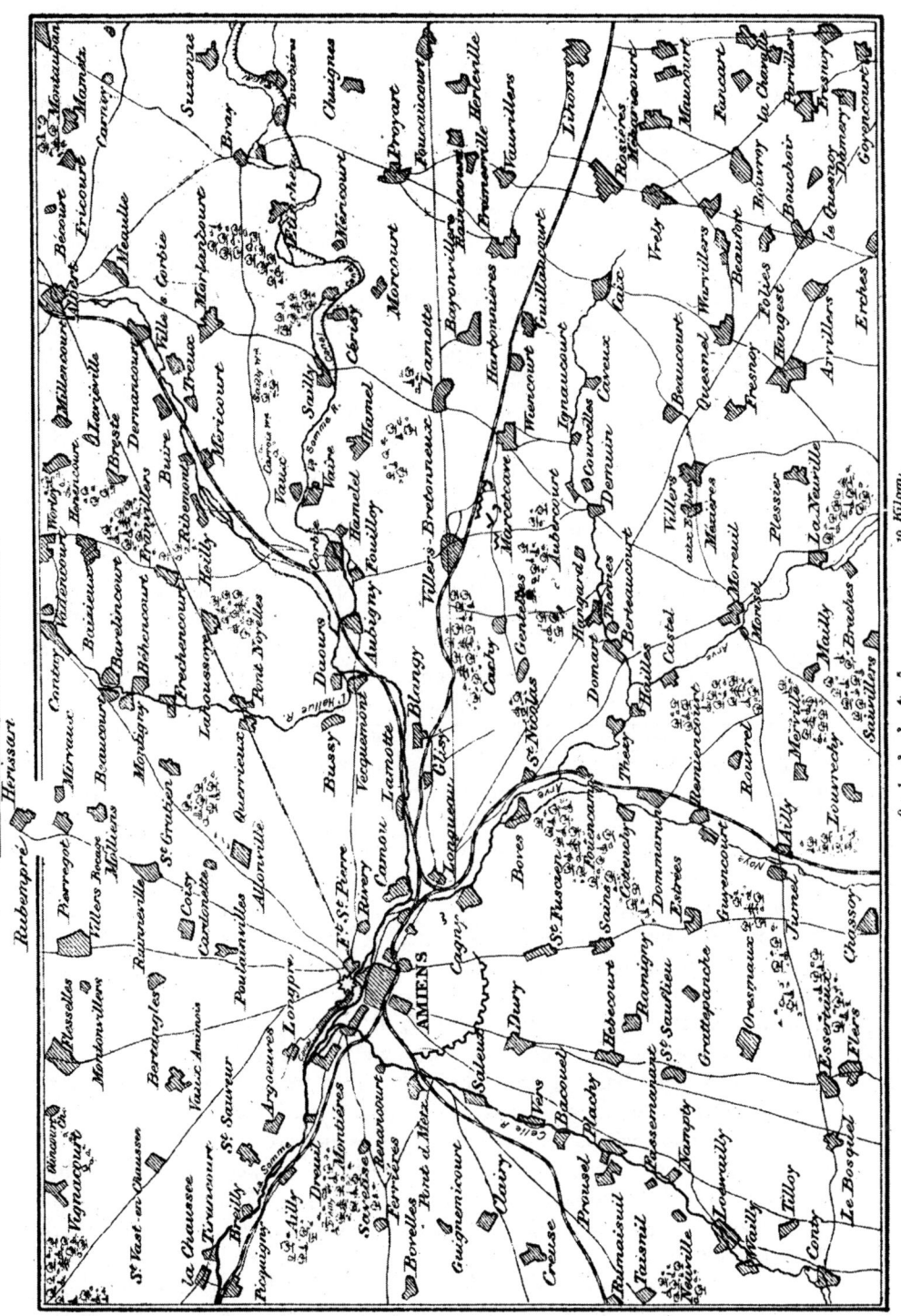

coast in order to come up with us. The Army of the North therefore had to face superior forces and so every effort had to be made to choose a good position in which to fight, one which had enough resources to accommodate the army in a very inclement season and simultaneously secure its provisioning. In addition, the enemy possession of the citadel had to be taken account of. The Prussian garrison had evacuated Amiens on the approach of the French army, but on leaving its commander had declared that if French troops entered the city it would be the signal for an all-out bombardment by the commandant of the citadel. The latter had begun to anticipate this threat. When the commanding general was reconnoitring the heights of the Noyon suburb, outside the town, accompanied only by General Farre, several unfortunate and unoffending inhabitants had been killed or wounded that afternoon near the citadel; public vehicles had even been fired on.

The French army posted itself on the right bank of the Somme, which presented a series of heights overlooking the left bank. There it was completely covered towards the south by the river and the canal, with their vast swamps which were very difficult to cross. All the bridges had been broken. A battle line was adopted which faced the citadel, the only point of passage left to the enemy, in the Hallue valley, where lay the villages of Daours, Bussy [-lès-Daours], Querrieux, Pont-Noyelles, Bavelincourt, Béhencourt, Vadencourt and Contay. The majority of the troops were billetted there. The rest occupied the length of the railway line by the town of Corbie, where headquarters was established, and the neighbouring villages.

At the same time, the completion and reinforcement of the several units was undertaken. In addition, a division of *Mobilisés* was called to the army. General Faidherbe therefore found himself at the head of four complete divisions, each having two brigades. In the first three divisions each brigade consisted of four line battalions and three of the *Garde Mobile*. The 4th Division alone contained *Gardes Nationales mobilisés*. The number of cannon was raised to 78, of which 12 were mountain pieces.

A plan for the organization of the army into two corps was accordingly submitted to the government, which approved it, and the formation of 23rd Corps was decreed. Colonels Derroja and du Bessol were appointed major generals to command the divisions. Generals Paulze d'Ivoy and Lecointe were made lieutenant generals to head 23rd and 22nd Corps respectively, and General Farre was advanced to the same grade in order to become chief of staff of the Army of the North, of which General Faidherbe was made commanding general (Appendix G). Lieutenant Colonel de Villenoisy was promoted colonel and assistant to the chief of staff.

Action of Querrieux, 20 December 1870

The 22nd Corps, General Lecointe, consisting of two divisions and six batteries, was posted from Daours to Contay along the Hallue. The 23rd Corps, General Paulze d'Ivoy, had its 1st Division (Admiral Moulac), containing the *fusiliers marins*, occupy Corbie and the neighbourhood, with three batteries and the two reserve batteries. The 2nd Division, *Mobilisés* of General Robin, whose two brigades were commanded by Colonels Brusley and Amos, occupied a second line in the villages southwest of Albert, covering the railway and detaching a regiment to Bray[-sur-Somme] to guard the line of the Somme between Péronne and Corbie.

The battle positions were carefully pointed out to each corps. The 1st Division of 23rd Corps was to occupy the commanding heights between Daours and Bussy, on the extreme left towards the Somme. The 2nd Division of 22nd Corps faced Pont-Noyelles, Querrieux and Fréchencourt, and finally the right up to the position at Contay was defended by the 1st Division of that corps, supported by the Robin Division, which faced Béhencourt. According to the instructions of the commanding general, the villages in the bottom of the valley were to be defended for but a short while by skirmishers. The main effort was to be made defending the rear positions. However, the villages could be reoccupied when the enemy had been repulsed from the heights, which it was thought they would attack in force.

We had just established ourselves in our billets when a strong enemy reconnoitring party, about 2,000 men with two cannon, moved on Querrieux, the centre of our position. Its movement was promptly reported by scouts. The 18th Chasseur Battalion and a battalion of the 33rd Line appeared in front of them and despite their superiority pushed them back to the Querrieux wood four kilometres away, forcing them to retreat speedily without giving our artillery time to support them. This very brisk combat cost us seven killed and 20 wounded. The enemy left 10 dead, 40 wounded and several prisoners, and also brought off 50 wounded in four wagons.

Battle of Pont-Noyelles, 22 December 1870

The following day [22 December] there were several outpost skirmishes, especially along the Somme, where the enemy seemed to be assembling his forces at Bray. This day was employed correcting the positions taken and preparing for the battle which appeared near. We had learned the enemy was in strength in the neighbourhood of the citadel, that he had built bridges at Camons and had occupied this village in force, and that he was only awaiting the arrival of new reinforcments to attack us. However, he still did not appear ready, and on the morning of the 23rd a start had just been made on several works to strengthen our positions when an attack began, much earlier than we had thought. Nonetheless, we were ready for one.

Around 9 a.m. the main guards in front of the Querrieux wood reported the appearance of strong Prussian columns issuing from Amiens, which were advancing on our positions by different routes. The corps were at once alerted and quickly took up their positions along the left bank of the Hallue. They had just been posted there when towards 11 the enemy fired his first cannon shots. Despite every efforts, the 1st Division of 23rd Corps could not arrive before 12:30 at Daours, on the left wing of the line of battle, because its billets were at some distance. As a result, the 2nd Division of 22nd Corps was initially very pressed, but the attack was nonetheless held. The villages along the Hallue were defended by detachments told off for that purpose, and they drew in the main guards, which fell back in order, firing.

The considerable masses of the enemy obliged us to abandon these villages practically all at once. Soon the action became general along a line which bent more than 12 kilometres from Daours to Contay. The heights on the right bank were crowned with an almost continuous line of enemy artillery, and they sent about 80 cannon against us. On the left bank, our batteries were more thinly spread, but the lines of skirmishers on the slopes presented an uninterrupted wall of fire which did not allow the enemy to advance.

The action reached a great height on the left near Daours. The sailors of Admiral Moulac held bravely under fire. The four batteries, two of which were of 12-pounders, which were on the plateau suffered much. Several cannon were put out action had were forced to retire in order to reorder themselves. Strong enemy columns entered Daours and followed our skirmishers closely.

At the same time, towards 3 p.m., the fight was just as heavy in the centre. The enemy massed in Querrieux and attempted to debouch towards Pont-Noyelles. They succeeded in climbing the slopes and were on the point of taking two of our cannons. But they were halted in time and pushed back to the river by a company of *Mobiles* of the Somme and Marne commanded by Captain d'Hauterive, and by the reserves of the 2nd Division, and were bombarded in Pont-Noyelles, which was burned. On the right, our artillery found favourable positions and fought with success against the enemy artillery without suffering much from it. The attempts of the enemy to debouch from Fréchencourt were fruitless. The *Mobiles* and a battalion of *Mobilisés* even took Béhencourt, but could not hold it. Last, on the extreme right the Derroja Division succeeded in preventing the enemy from advancing, as much as from the good work of its artillery as from the good positions it occupied. It kept two battalions on the right bank of the river to threaten the enemy left.

At 4 p.m. it was decided to attempt a general attack on the villages, while at the same time on the extreme right the 1st Division would execute a turning movement with the troops on the right bank of the river. This movement had no more than limited success, since night fell too quickly and did not permit it to be pushed far enough. The attack on Bavelincourt succeeded completely and the 1st Division of 22nd Corps held the village. Pont-Noyelles and Daours were assaulted with the greatest vigour, and the commanding general was persuaded that we were the victors, having himself left Daours at night, where he left Admiral Moulac with several battalions. But in the midst of the confusion caused by a gloomy night, the Prussians remained in the houses in great numbers, supported by strong detachments which outflanked the villages in silence, took them almost without fighting and captured about 200 men in each of them. Despite these incidents, which were not known until the night, our troops occupied the positions which we had chosen and as a result believed themselves the victors. They were given to understand that in wartime a victory is gained when one bivouacs on the field of battle and that there could be no question of their returning to their billets, several miles in the rear. The army therefore camped during a dark night and a temperature of -7 to -8° [19 to 17° F], without wood to make fires and with frozen bread as its sole food.

This cruel test was supported with a patience and abnegation which one could not sufficiently admire, and which brought as much honour to our young soldiers as their courage under enemy fire. At daybreak of the following day all the troops were in line, the ammunition had been replenished from our reserves and we were ready to continue the fight. But the enemy did not wish to do so, even though Prince Albert of Saxony had arrived with reinforcements. All that occurred were several shots from skirmishers at some distance from the two lines and several cannon shots from our extreme right by the division of *Mobilisés*, towards the villages and the wood, where enemy troops were visible.

Because of the extreme cold and the excessive fatigues which our soldiers had undergone, it could not be thought of to impose on them a second night in bivouac, and at 2 p.m. the commanding general decided to send the troops to their billets. This movement was carried out in perfect order, without disturbance from the enemy.

The losses we suffered in the battle of Pont-Noyelles were not that large, 141 dead, five of whom were officers, and 905 wounded, 45 of whom were officers, several hundred prisoners and a thousand missing. In addition, the artillery had lost 138 horses killed. The majority of the missing were from the *Garde Nationale mobilisé*, who left more because of the privations and weariness of the two previous days than out of fear of the enemy. Many soon rejoined their units, and each day several more came in. Examples were made of the officers; the guilty ones were dismissed. As to the enemy loss, there were only a small number of prisoners, but the most moderate figures account for several thousand men put out of action by the dropping fire of our skirmishers and the artillery on the villages and woods they occupied. The town of Amiens was encumbered with numerous wounded.

We had held the Prussians in a battle at Pont-Noyelles and had saved Le Havre, but we could not think about doing anything more for the moment. Our green troops were still somewhat disorganized after several days of marching and combat. The enemy, who had fallen back on Amiens and its citadel, could receive reinforcements from Normandy, and especially from Paris, which they thought necessary to crush us. The commanding general believed it necessary to find safer billets along the right bank of the Scarpe, between Arras and Douai, to give the men several days of much-needed rest and profit by the advantages this position gave to restock the army with the supplies it needed so much. The enemy army followed us during this march, but German accounts are wrong to say that they *pursued* us.

The position chosen by the commanding general for the cantonment of the army was behind the Scarpe, the right adjoining Arras and the left Douai. The troops were established in a first line in the villages of Fampoux, Rœux, Vitry[-en-Artois], Brebières and Corbehem, and in a second line from Oppy to Esquerchin there was placed the 2nd Division of 23rd Corps. As a result a very strong and well-supported position was occupied, where an attack by superior forces could be resisted. But the enemy did not try to seek the Army of the North; they contented themselves with sending scouts around Arras and up to the Lens road. As a result, in the skirts of this town a battalion of *Mobilisés* camped at Souchez and not part of the Army of the North was dispersed and partly captured by a troop of 20 lancers which had ventured to the rear of our lines at Arras at a distance of more than 20 kilometres. It is, however, true that these *Mobilisés* had no cartridges.

Action of Achiet-le-Grand, 2 January 1871

By 31 December these incursions had been stopped by a strong column which reconnoitred west of Arras. The following day, the army left its position and posted itself in front of this town from Rivière to Tilly. On the 2nd [January 1871], in order to counter the bombardment of Péronne, of which news had just arrived, we set ourselves in motion by four parallel routes towards the enemy forces which had assembled in the region of Bapaume and Bucquoy. The 1st Division of 22nd Corps arrived at Bucquoy and Achiet-le-Petit without hindrance.

The 2nd Division, with the commanding general, reported the enemy to be at Ablainzevelle and speedily moved from that village towards Achiet-le-Grand, which was occupied by 2,000 men with three cannon, who were dislodged after a brisk battle. They were then chased out of Bihucourt and pursued to the neighbourhood of Bapaume. In this affair the enemy suffered serious losses and left in our hands 50 prisoners, one of whom was an officer; we had a hundred killed or wounded.

Action of Béhagnies, 2 January 1871

During this time, the 1st Division of 22nd Corps, commanded by Post-Captain Payen, who had succeeded Admiral Moulac with the title of general in the auxiliary army, had passed through without opposition the villages of Boyelles and Ervillers, along the high road to Bapaume. Debouching from Ervillers, it was told that the enemy was occupying a very strong position at the village of Béhagnies. The peasants asserted they were few in number; the advance guard of the 19th Chasseur Battalion and a section of artillery began an attack. It was repulsed by a violent rifle and artillery fire. All the units of the division, which were deployed to support the assault, took part, opposing strong forces whose presence had not been suspected, and the fight went on into the afternoon with great violence. Our troops entered the first houses in the village, but attempts to outflank it on the left did not succeed in the face of the enemy's numerous cavalry, which found itself faced by green infantry. The troops could not stay in the position and, supported by the fire of the reserves and artillery, returned to Ervillers, where they established themselves for the night without being attacked. The arrival of the 2nd Division (*Mobilisés*) of General Robin would have changed the nature of the fight, if it had come into line more quickly, as its orders dictated. It advanced without little loss into the village of Mory, where it was not without effect on the conduct of the enemy.

After the occupation of Achiet-le-Grand and Bihucourt by 22nd Corps had made the position of Béhagnies and Sapignies no longer tenable by the Prussian army, it abandoned these places during the night and moved to the rear onto a line formed by the villages of Grévillers, Biefvillers[-lès-Bapaume], Favreuil and Beugnâtre, thus covering the approaches to Bapaume.

Battle of Bapaume, 3 January 1871

On the morning of 3 January we began the attack against the centre of the position, to where General Faidherbe went. The 2nd Division of 22nd Corps, General du Bessol, attacked Biefvillers, while the 1st Division, General Derroja, went towards Grevillers. For its part, the 1st Division of 23rd Corps, Commandant Payen, entered Béhagnies and Sapignies without firing a shot and then advanced towards the strongly garrisoned Favreuil, which it bombarded from two sides. The 2nd Division (General Robin) took only a minor role in the action, deriving no more advantage than covering the extreme left wing by its presence.

The villages were defended very stubbornly by the enemy. The fight was especially fierce at Biefvillers, which was not taken until after several attacks and until it had been outflanked on the left by the troops of General du Bessol, while General Derroja supported the attack on the right by speedily capturing Grevillers. We found Biefvillers and the road leading to Avesnes covered with dead and wounded Prussians. The houses of Avesnes were filled with them, and a fairly large number of prisoners remained in our hands.

The artillery, which was brought up between the two villages, had to sustain a terrible struggle with the artillery the enemy had accumulated near Bapaume, on the Albert road. At length the batteries of Captains Collignon, Bocquillon and Giron succeeded, not without loss, in suppressing the enemy fire, and a general advance was made on Bapaume. The small village of Avesnes was taken at a rush by the 1st Division. A head of a column from the 2nd Division, carried away by its ardour, assaulted the Arras suburb [of Bapaume] at the same time, but was stopped at the entrance to the town.

A vast irregular esplanade, with ditches mostly filled, had replaced the ancient ramparts of the fortress and presented serious obstacles to the movements of an attacker, who was exposed to fire from the walls and loopholed houses. It was necessary to destroy with artillery the places where they had lodged, a very hard thing to do to a French town and to which the commanding general could not resign himself, not being convinced of the necessity of taking Bapaume. During this time, General Lecointe reported that the village of Tilloy [Ligny-Thilloy], which was on our right wing, had been occupied by the enemy, and that a Prussian column with cannon was advancing from there along the Albert road. This attempt to turn our right wing had to be opposed, and the brigade of Colonel Pittié was immediately sent against Tilloy, which it captured only after the stiffest resistance and which it held. On the left wing, General Paulze d'Ivoy had no less success against the village of Favreuil.

The Robin Division, which stayed largely in the rear, was replaced by two battalions of the 2nd Brigade of the Payen Division, which were for the attack on the right wing joined only by a battalion of *voltigeurs mobilisés*; at the same time the brigade of Colonel de la Grange attacked the centre. Together these troops forced the enemy barricades and took all his positions. The attack was supported on the Arras road at Bapaume by a battery from the 2nd Division of 22nd Corps, and the enemy fell back in full retreat.

When night fell, therefore, we were therefore victorious along the entire line. The fight continued weakly on the extreme right, where the enemy tried hard to hold the village of Ligny [Ligny-Thilloy]. The night was passed in the villages taken from the enemy. General Faidherbe would have billetted the troops there for several days, but they were choked with dead and wounded. Fresh attacks were possible, since the battlefield was so close to Amiens, where the enemy had more forces. In addition, we learned the assault on Péronne had been suspended and that the siege artillery had been withdrawn from there and that on 31 December and 1 January not a shot had been fired on the town. However, it was not known that two cannon on the left bank [of the Somme] had resumed firing. Taking into consideration the exhaustion of the troops and the extreme cold which they had had to bear, the commanding general decided to retake the billets a few kilometres to the rear, postponing for a few days the march on Péronne if it became necessary. In consequence, at 4 a.m. we moved off for these billets.

Our success at Bapaume had cost the enemy very considerable losses. The information which we received indicated several thousand killed and wounded; moreover, some units in the battle had fallen apart and had streamed in disorder towards Amiens. In an order of the day from General von Goeben reproduced in German and British papers, he ordered unit commanders to point out any officers who had fled the battle of Bapaume in order that they might be immediately dismissed (Appendix H).

The Prussians have stated that they had forces very close in strength to ours. They had brought up units besieging Péronne, and they received reinforcements up to the end of the battle. They certainly had more than 20,000 men, and a nearly equal number on our side were effectively engaged.

During the night of the 3rd and the following morning they evacuated Bapaume, convinced we were going to attack them and believing they were not strong enough to hold the town. At the same time they sent two squadrons of white cuirassiers to reconnoitre. These squadrons wanted to attack the rearguard of a brigade of the du Bessol Division. The rearguard, which consisted of chasseurs, fired when they were within 50 paces, practically destroying one of the squadrons, the other fleeing. On the evening of the 4th, thinking we were two miles away, the Prussians re-entered Bapaume.

The losses of the Army of the North in the battle of Bapaume were 183 killed, nine of whom were officers, 1,136 wounded, of whom 41 were officers, and 800 missing, among them three officers. The losses were especially grave in the 1st Division of 22nd Corps when it attacked Béhagnies on 2 January. The missing men only fled to the rear, because the enemy did not take any prisoners on the 3rd.

Bombardment and capitulation of Péronne, 18 December 1870 to 10 January 1871

We have stated that after having beaten the Prussians in front of Bapaume on 3 January, the Army of the North took up again its billets around Boileux [Boisleux-aux-Mont], the first railway station between Arras and Amiens. As soon as it had been reprovisioned, the army moved forward in order to ascertain the situation of Péronne, about whose fate it had not been sufficiently apprised. On the 10th it cantoned around Ervillers. Thirty-four *francs-tireurs* under Captain Delaporte and Lieutenant Denal took 43 lancers and their horses in a farm after having killed the commander and wounded several men. Following their usual practice, the Prussians avenged themselves pitilessly on the village, which had nothing to do with the incident. In the night of the 10th/11th, the Derroja Division surprised and captured the main Prussian guards of Béhagnies and Sapignies. On the 11th the same division entered Bapaume, which the troops of Generals von Kummer and Goeben had just evacuated. There we learned to our great astonishment of the capitulation of Péronne to General von Barnekow.

We can do no better than to present the following information about this capitulation, taken from a note by Sub-Prefect M. Blondin.

Péronne, a *city never conquered* [original in Latin], according to the motto which it now is necessary to erase from its crest, had been a very strong place during the period when regular sieges were common. It had considerable natural defences. The Somme sufficed to protect it in certain places, its advanced works were wisely placed, and all its fortifications were perfectly traced. Much work was necessary in order to place the town in a state of defence. M. Payre, a retired commandant of engineers, was prodigiously active in this regard. The armament was admittedly incomplete, for many of pieces lacked carriages, but carriages were constructed in Péronne. We had very few rifled cannon, but at the same time that a company of *fusiliers marins* arrived there came two naval guns, which were placed under a cover which was skilfully constructed. The artillery and engineers united their efforts, and when the time came the fortress was in a state in which to resist.

The Prussians approached. Their insolence revealed itself in an audacious attempt: a young lieutenant presented himself as a parliamentary and summoned the fortress to surrender in the name of an imaginary general. From considerations of respect he was allowed to leave. It was attempting the impossible: "I had 12 troopers," he said laughingly in the inns of the neighbouring villages, "if I had had 24 the place would have been mine." The demand was presented again some days later by a captain from the same regiment (7th Lancers of the Rhine), who was accompanied by a lieutenant and the trumpeter prescribed by custom. He left outside our lines 20 troopers, who scattered around the fortress in order to reconnoitre our positions map in hand. He also summoned the town to surrender. However, these officers were less fortunate than their predecessor; they were held prisoner in Péronne because they had none of the regulation characteristics of parliamentaries. Later it was known with certainty that their approach had been equally a bluff.

We then had several false alarms. When, however, after the battle of Bapaume the Army of the North retreated in order to take up its billets, the situation became very clear. On 27 December the investment began. Scouting parties sent in different directions returned to Péronne pursued closely by superior forces. In the distance columns could be seen moving rapidly behind the heights which dominate the fortress on all sides. These heights, which range from 1,000 to 2,000 metres, have the particular characteristic that their slopes facing away from the town are fairly steep, forming a barrier against the fire of the fortress and providing natural positions for enemy batteries. But the batteries placed there could not reach the ramparts, which were well covered. However, it was well to think of ramparts when the Prussians were the enemy! They made war neither on the defences nor the defenders, but on property and an inoffensive population, on helpless old men, women and children! The bombardment of Péronne, in this campaign so full of feats of this sort, is perhaps one of the best and most odious examples of the calm and methodical ferocity which the generals of King Wilhelm have introduced into the practices of war.

At noon on 28 December a parliamentary appeared, bearing a demand (written this time) from General von Senten, which ran along these lines: "The Army of the North has retreated to behind Arras, my troops have surrounded the fortress of Péronne on all sides. I summon you to surrender, declaring that I have the means to compel you to do so and will hold you responsible for all the misfortunes which a bombardment will inflict on the civilian population." To which the commandant of Péronne responded: "I have but one reply to make to your summons: the government of my country has placed the fortress of Péronne under my command and I will defend it to the last gasp. I throw back on you the responsibility for all the misfortunes which, by your account and contrary to the practices of war between civilized nations, you will inflict on a peaceful population."

The bombardment was to begin at 2 p.m., but we had not taken account of the difference in time, and our parliamentary had not yet returned when the enemy opened fire, without giving us time to alert the population. Nine field batteries under the command of Colonel Kamecki, the same man who presided over the bombardment of Paris, were employed in this attack. This at least is what was written to the *Daily Telegraph* by a German reporter who entered Péronne on 10 January when the Prussians were victorious. The enemy fire, to which we could not make an effective reply, was concentrated on the buildings of the town itself, which was 20 hectares in size, sparing the suburbs and not hitting the defenses. For about 24 hours it raged with incredible violence. The first target was the church, and then the hospital (naturally), which was marked by the Red Cross flag. The saving of the sick took place under a rain of shells and with a rare luck, thanks to the courage of the nuns and several brave citizens, whose number was unfortunately too small. The fire having then been lifted, the shells passed two to three metres above our heads. We therefore had only to fear the effects of ricochets, and the transferral of the sick from the hospital to a safe barracks was accomplished without loss. It goes without saying that the burning of the hospital buildings had no effect but to increase the Prussian fire; shells fell continuously on all sides to prevent help being rendered.

Such deeds cannot be qualified; to denounce them is to diminish them. However, once more, among the so serious and numerous affronts to the rights of man and the practice of civilized nations which the Geneva Convention had set out, I do not believe that there will be found any more cynical and revolting! The civilian population was terrified; every house was hit in turn. After 24 hours of this intense and incessant fire, the enemy's ammunition ran out. There were then several hours of calm. On the following day the fire was slightly less intense, but it continued without interruption until the end of the day on 30 December. On the 31st and 1 January, there was a complete cessation of hostilities. This was caused by the Army of the North, which was on the march towards Bapaume, as we afterwards knew. The Prussians made preparations to receive it. During the evening of 2 January and all through the 3rd cannon fire could be heard from the direction of Bapaume.

The abrupt disappearance of the Prussian batteries was explained by the fact that they belonged to an army corps on the march towards the north and had thought to *pick up* Péronne in passing. What remained, several rifled 12-pounders, several howitzers and 22-pounder mortars on the left bank of the Somme, could have been taken by a successful sortie. None was made. The bombardment recommenced around 10 a.m. on the 2nd and continued without fury but also without letup. Hope vanished that help would come from the Army of the North; we believed it to be in retreat ... and events would show us that by a combination of disastrous circumstances it was mistaken about our situation. Finally, on the 9th, 70 houses having been completely destroyed, 500 to 600 more rendered more or less uninhabitable and several others barely intact, a parliamentary arrived in front of the outposts. He bore a letter from General von Barnekow which announced the arrival of fresh forces and a considerable amount of siege artillery and proposed honourable terms if the fortress wished to capitulate, at the same time threatening a bombardment with large-calibre weapons if resistance continued.

The council of defence which met decided to renew a request which would permit the non-combatant population to leave. This request was denied, as it had been the first time, and the council was forced to give its views about a surrender. It was composed of the unit commanders. In the discussion, M. Payre opposed the majority opinion in advocating the most stubborn defence: "Our defences are intact; not a gun has been dismounted. The bombardment cannot cause much harm any longer; the worst has been done and it will not help them. This is not military rhetoric. Péronne is the key to the Somme, and its possession could be most important for either of the two armies in the region." This was his argument. It was strongly supported by Sub-Prefect M. Blondin, but unfortunately it had no weight, and after taking a vote Commandant Garnier resigned himself to surrender (Appendix I).

Reflections on the capitulation of Péronne

On 15 December General Faidherbe had written to the commandant of Péronne to urge him not to repeat the examples of weakness which had been given by several other commandants of fortresses and saying that while the Army of the North was in the field he could count on its support. Faced with this unexpected surrender, and with a protest from a certain number of officers from the garrison, among whom was M. Poitevin, a navy lieutenant and commander of the *fusiliers marins*, he requested the minister of war to order an inquest about the conduct of the commandant of Péronne. This surrender was variously received by the public, and gave rise to polemics in opposition newspapers. The defenders of the commandant claimed that, given the fashion of the Prussians in attacking towns by bombarding and burning them, commandants would be inhumane to prolong a defence at the cost of the ruin and destruction of a civilian population which was too large to find shelter from the shells which fell on it, despite the fact that the commandants' walls and garrisons were intact.

However, the regulation for troops in the field is rigid: Article 218. — Military law sentences to death any commandant who delivers up his fortress without having forced the besieger to carry on the siege by slow and continuing works and at least having repulsed one assault *of his force in practicable breaches.*

To which the response was: but this rule assumes that the enemy attacks the works of a fortress and makes breaches in it, and the Prussians did nothing like that! This is a paradox: the Prussians would have certainly been forced to have done so in order to capture the garrison and its equipment and provisions — which was certainly their ultimate goal — if a surrender had not taken place when they had more or less destroyed the town by a bombardment. In making this case their methods are evidently justified in principle contrary to the generosity and even loyalty which practices demand, if not sanctified by written agreements, at least implicitly admitted and generally respected by civilized peoples. Their system has succeeded so well in France that they have been authorized to state that humanity had been served. Taking Péronne as an example, they could state that: we have become the victors by a bombardment which killed 20 inhabitants and by several hundred killed and wounded on our side (assuming they had suffered these losses), whereas if we had besieged and taken the town according to the previous rules of war it would perhaps have cost us 3,000 to 4,000 men and the besieged 1,000 to 1,500. In addition, if such sieges had been made the war would have become very lengthy and might perhaps still be in progress! It is to be understood that this specious reasoning would not be possible if a town which resigned itself to complete ruin forced the enemy to follow up the bombardment with a siege in form. The besieger would not find any advantage in the destruction of the civilian population and would be obliged to renounce his odious system under the pressure of universal execration.

Be that as it may, if the commandants of fortresses have to surrender from motives of humanity, it is necessary that the regulation be changed immediately; duty must be clearly defined. And if the regulation is changed and if fortresses are no longer held to defend themselves, it will be necessary to avoid keeping garrisons, artillery, ammunition and provisions in them, since such things would be gifts assembled in advance to present lovingly to an enemy.

We consider as unfortunate for the future the unchivalrous methods the Prussians had used in this war. It could be said that they had followed the example of the revolutionaries of Paris [i.e., the Paris Commune]. They had systematically pillaged wine cellars, employed hostages, burned homes, monuments, churches, libraries (Strasbourg), even by petroleum, replacing the hot shot with which the Austrians had burned Lille in 1792, and last took reprisals on innocent inhabitants when some unfortunate accident occurred in their village. Do not we see here the germs of all the crimes committed by certain revolutionaries in Paris, who without taking the same line as the Prussian staff had pushed this system to its last limits, as must do desperate men in whom, alas! no human sentiment remained, and for the majority of whom the family no longer existed.

Action of Vermand, 18 January 1871

Now let us return to the operations of the Army of the North. On 14 January, continuing its advance, it entered Albert, which the Prussians had abandoned on our approach, and bivouacked in the neighbourhood. On the 15th reconnaissances were made to Bray [-sur-Somme], Hailly [Heilly] and Bouzincourt.

It was known for certain that the enemy, assuming we wished to force a passage over the Somme, had cut down or blown up the last bridges and barricaded the villages on its left bank. At the same time, in case we tried to cross the Somme between Corbie and Amiens, they had made great preparations for defence along the line of the Hallue, principally at Pont-Noyelles, on the battlefield of 22 December. They had even placed part of the artillery of Amiens behind earthworks. We could not think of forcing a passage over the Somme below Amiens in the presence of an army at least somewhat stronger than our own, entrenched as it was and with the ability to receive reinforcements very quickly. On the other hand, we could not remain inactive.

We were aware that the garrison of Paris was about to make a grand and supreme effort. A telegram from Bordeaux sent by M. de Freycinet in the absence of M. Gambetta, informed General Faidherbe that the moment for vigorous action had come; he especially requested us to draw on us from Paris as many forces as possible. General Faidherbe, strongly convinced of this necessity, believed that he would attain this end in freeing himself from the army in front of him by forced marches towards the east and southeast in order to speedily arrive south of Saint-Quentin, where he would threaten the railway line from La Fère through Chauny, Noyon and Compiègne. It was certain to soon encounter considerable forces, but the time to act had come and he could hope to have the time, if threatened by superior forces, to retire towards the north, drawing them after him and to await them under the protection of the fortresses of Cambrai, Bouchain, Douai and even Valenciennes, where he could hold them if they dared to attack whatever their strength.

We therefore left Albert on the 16th for Sailly-Saillisel and the other villages around Combles. The roads had been made somewhat slippery by black ice and the march was thereby made so hard that the troops did not arrive in their billets until very late. The following day we went towards Vermand. The 2nd Brigade of the Derroja Division dislodged from the wood of Buire, near Templeux [-la-Fosse], several battalions of the von Barnekow Division which had occupied that feature in order to prevent our passage. In the afternoon a Prussian detachment of all arms left Vermand on the approach of the 1st Brigade of the same division. Two squadrons of dragoons pursued them.

On the 18th we were attacked strongly while continuing our march in the direction of Saint-Quentin. At 10 a.m. the tail of the du Bessol Division was harassed by cavalry from the von den Groeben Division. At noon it was attacked near Beauvois [-en-Vermandois] by the advance guard of the von Kummer Division. This showed that General von Goeben had put his entire army in motion to follow us by forced marches, at the same time calling up reinforcements from all sides. A charge by hussars on a battalion of *Mobiles* of Gard was repulsed in a decided manner by a battalion of *Mobiles* of Somme and Marne under Colonel de Brouard.

General du Bessol, who had arrived at Roupy with his 2nd Brigade, went back with a battalion and four cannon in order to disengage his 1st Brigade. However, this had already been done by the Payen Division of 22nd Corps, which had marched to the sound of the guns from Vermand towards Caulaincourt and Trefcon and took them from the enemy. The du Bessol Division thereupon resumed its march towards the billets south of Saint-Quentin indicated for it.

The 1st Brigade of the Payen Division, Lieutenant Colonel Michelet, with the *fusiliers marins*, broke the first attempt of the enemy, and it was soon reinforced by the 2nd Brigade, Commandant de la Grange. General Paulze d'Ivoy, seeing that considerable forces were engaging him, the von Kummer and von den Groeben divisions, was forced to halt in consequence. He occupied with infantry the wood between Caulaincourt and Vermand and posted the Dupuich battery on the plateau to the north of this wood. In this position he repulsed the enemy and held until nightfall. The 2nd Division, that of the *Mobilisés* of General Robin, marched to the sound of the guns and took part in the end of the engagement. This division was left in part in Vermand during the night, whereas the Payen Division took up its billets in Saint-Quentin itself.

The fight of Vermand cost us perhaps 500 men killed or wounded. Only heavy enemy losses can explain the fact that they did not make more vigorous efforts in front of Vermand. The Prussians claimed to have taken one of our cannon this day. They recovered it from the bottom of a village pond, where it had been sunk by the clumsiness of a driver and where it had been abandoned only after vigorous but useless attempts in order not to retard the march of the column.

The events of the 18th proved that the concentration of Prussian forces was already far too advanced to allow a march towards the north in order to have the support of the fortresses. Battle about Saint-Quentin had to be accepted. By a happy coincidence, this was the same day the Army of Paris fought at Montretout.

Battle of Saint-Quentin, 19 January 1871

The general situation was not bad. With the resources of a great city close by, excellent positions were found for fighting on the heights which surround Saint-Quentin at a distance of three or four kilometres. The reason for the advance of the Prussian army, as had been forecast, was because General von Goeben, on learning of the recapture of Saint-Quentin on the 15th by Colonel Isnard (Appendix J), had exaggerated the importance of this deed. He did not know that Colonel Isnard had but a weak force almost entirely composed of *Gardes Mobiles*, and he believed there must be considerable forces around Saint-Quentin even before he knew of our movement towards there.

The troops were ordered to be ready at daybreak in the positions designated for them. Our force amounted to nearly 40,000 men. The 23rd Corps, reinforced by the Isnard Brigade, posted itself in an arc, its back to the town, its left by the mill of Rocourt and its right at the village of Fayet, extending along the canal of Saint-Quentin towards Cambrai. By a reversal its 1st Division (Payen) formed the left and its 2nd Division (*Mobilisés* Robin) the right. The Isnard Brigade was between them. The 22nd Corps was on the other side of the canal from Gauchy to Grugis [Grugies] up to the Paris road, facing south. Our army therefore formed a semi-circle around Saint-Quentin to its south and west. The enemy had to come up with the 23rd Corps by the Péronne and Ham roads, and with the 22nd Corps in the south by the Chauny (Paris) and La Fère roads. The lines of retreat were the Cambrai road through Le Catelet and the Le Cateau [-Cambrésis] road through Bohain [-en-Vermandois]. The Pauly Brigade (*Mobilisés* of Pas-du-Calais) at Bellicourt was to protect the lines of retreat.

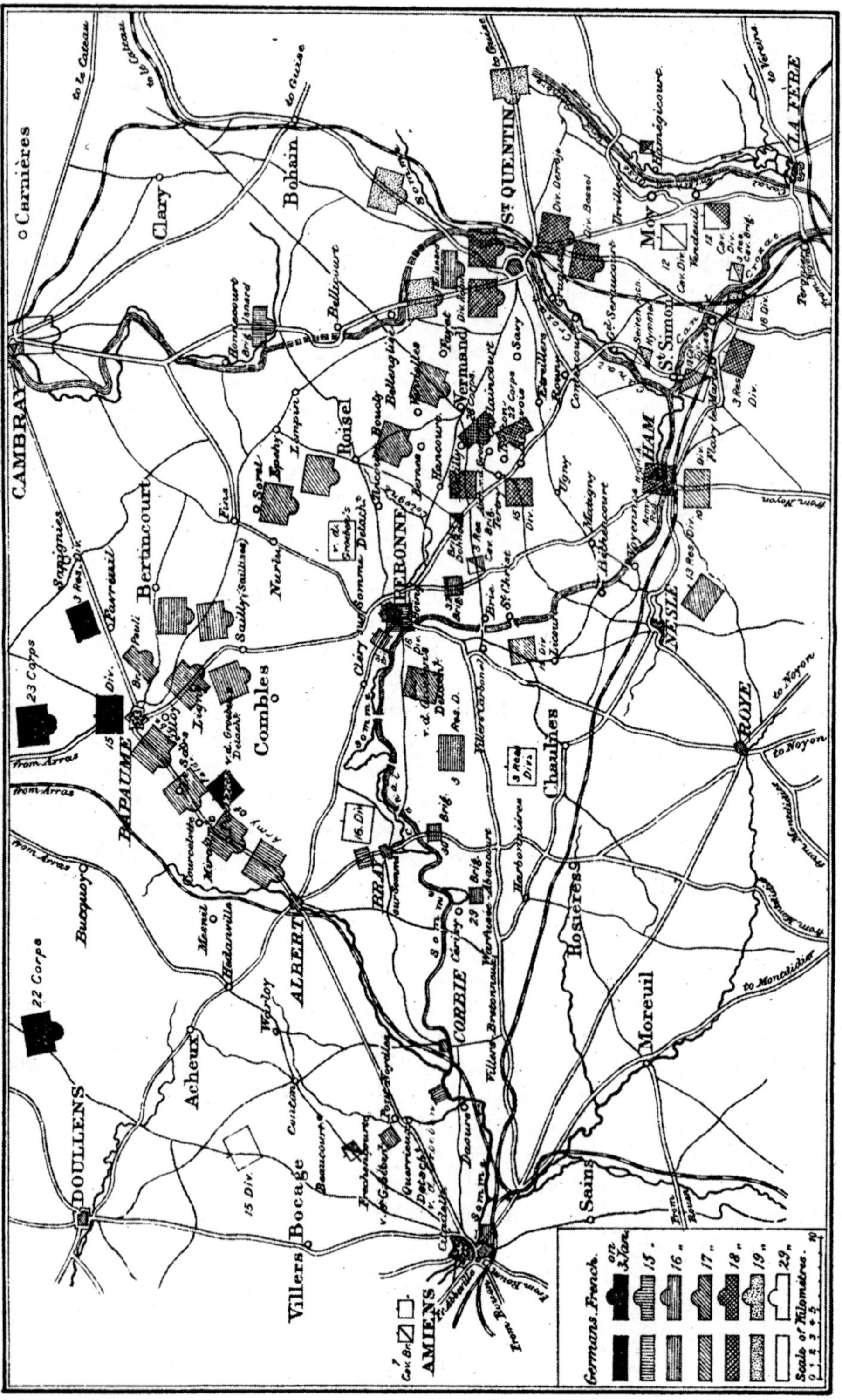

BATTLES ROUND BAPAUME & St QUENTIN.

After the beginning of the battle, a squadron of our dragoons had an engagement with a regiment of Prussian cavalry near Savy, during which Lieutenant Colonel Baussin received a cruel sabre cut to the head and we had 15 wounded. The Halphen battery had taken an excellent position to the left of Francilly, and it fought in a remarkable manner during the entire day. The Dupuich (Appendix K) and Dieudonné batteries established themselves in the rear of the right of the Robin Division in order to defend the Cambrai road, by where it was feared the enemy was attempting to turn our right and cut off our retreat. This was in fact the intention of General von Goeben.

The reserve batteries were placed to the left of the 23rd Corps on the heights which dominated the Ham road. It was to Ham that the railway brought a force of troops from Amiens and Rouen. The railway could also transport them from La Fère up to several kilometres from the battlefield.

During the first part of the day the fight consisted of no more than an affair of skirmishers and artillery for possession of the woods and villages between the two armies. But towards 2 p.m. enemy reinforcements arriving from Péronne attacked our extreme right in a vigorous manner and took Fayet from the Robin Division, by that means threatening the Cambrai road. The 1st Brigade of Commandant Payen, sent there, briskly retook the village, under the protection of a battery and a half from the artillery reserve which had been sent by the commanding general. At the same time, the Pauly Brigade of the *Mobilisés* of Pas-du-Calais, marching from Bellicourt to the sound of the guns, took the most honourable part in this operation. The Prussians were pushed back from the village, which the 48th *Mobiles* occupied and held until night. The other troops took post to the rear on the heights, where were positioned the Dupuich and Dieudonné batteries, and prevented the enemy from from moving towards the Cambrai road.

On the left, the Isnard and de la Grange brigades, displaying great valour, several times penetrated into the wood of Savy. But around 4 p.m., due to the arrival of the Memerly Division of the I Prussian Corps, they found themselves faced by too superior forces and were forced to give up the ground piece by piece. General Paulze d'Ivoy received from the commanding general orders to send reinforcements to the left in order to stop the progress of the enemy along the Ham road. Despite this, however, the enemy soon was able to advance along the road and along the canal, and they were halted only by the fire from the solid barricades in the Saint-Martin suburb, until the beginning of the fast-approaching night. Major Richard of the engineers, the senior aide-de-camp to the commanding general, remained at this barricade until nightfall in order to hold up the enemy as long as possible, but he was surrounded and could not make his escape without being several times taken and freeing himself from the Prussians by revolver fire. At nightfall, as on the east as on the south, our troops worn out by an entire day of combat preceded by three days of forced marches and skirmishes and by dreadful weather and roads, were ejected from Saint-Quentin by an enemy whose numbers were increasing every second through reinforcements which came from Rouen, Amiens, Péronne, Ham, Laon and La Fère and finally from Beauvais and Paris. A retreat was ordered for 22nd Corps along the Le Cateau road, for 23rd Corps along that of Cambrai.

The commanding general and his staff, having followed 22nd Corps as far as Essigny [-le-Petit], took with the cavalry the inbetween route. The heads of the Prussian columns entered Saint-Quentin by the La Fère and Ham roads, firing several shells into the town and capturing all the soldiers who had deserted, were lost or lame and several companies which had been surrounded. There remained in their hands three or four small mountain guns which were in the Isle suburb and two 4-pounders abandoned in the town itself. This artillery belonged to the small auxiliary columns which had entered Saint-Quentin at daybreak. However, the fifteen field batteries of the Army of the North were taken away intact to Cambrai, with their caissons and our convoy (Appendix L).

According to our information, the enemy must have had 5,000 men put out of action, and we but 3,000 during the 18th and 19th in the fights at Vermand and Saint-Quentin (Appendix M). This is accounted for by the fact that our fire hit masses of troops twice our size. Thanks to the stragglers which the enemy collected on the roads on the 20th and 21st, more than 6,000 prisoners should have fallen into his hands following the battle, most of them *Mobiles* and *Mobilisés*, but the majority escaped and rejoined their corps after several days (Appendix N).

On the 20th a Prussian detachment, pursuing our columns, arrived at the gates of Cambrai and in vain summoned the town to surrender. Another unit went to shell Landrecies but was repulsed by the artillery of that place. The enemy fell back accordingly towards Saint-Quentin, and they were confined to the limits of the department of the Somme by the armistice which was proclaimed on the 29th. Its conditions, as far as they concerned the Army of the North, were discussed at Amiens by Colonel de Villenoisy and General von Goeben, who showed the greatest courtesy. Unfortunately, owing to a higher order, we were forced to give up Abbeville, which the Bauboin Brigade had succeeded in holding against several Prussian attempts. General Faidherbe was only able to secure the concession that the town would not be subjected to forced contributions. The exchange of 600 to 700 prisoners in our hands, 30 of whom were officers, took place.

The Army of the North, billeted after the battle of Saint-Quentin around the towns of Cambrai, Douai, Valenciennes, Arras and Lille, rapidly reorganized. By 10 February it could report a strength almost equal to that which it fought at Saint-Quentin, thanks to the incorporation of several thousand *Mobilisés* and the activity of the several arms (the administration of the Northern Railway, M. de Saint-Didier at its head, in these circumstances displayed the most commendable eagerness to expedite the movements of troops and equipment, as it had done throughout the war), which an appearance of M. Gambetta at the end of January had brought on. The fact that the commanding general von Goeben knew very well that his fourth battle had not reduced the Army of the North to impotence is proved by the inclusion in his order of the 21st (Appendix O), which ordered Lieutenant Generals von Kummer, von Barnekow and von den Groeben to observe Cambrai and Arras of an indication of their lines of retreat towards Amiens and Péronne *in case they were pressed by the French army.*

This Army of the North, which had fought four battles and several fights with the enemy within two months, had suffered losses which one could estimate without exaggeration at more than 15,000 men. But it was as numerous and more experienced than before (a little disillusioned, it is true), when by an order of the minister of war on 15 February 1871 the 22nd Corps, 18,000 men strong with 10 batteries (two 12-, two 8- and six 4-pounder), was embarked at Dunkirk under the care of Post Captain Périgot, the chief officer of the naval region of the North, to join the army at Cherbourg (Appendix P). The 23rd Corps, formed largely of sailors, *Mobiles* and *Mobilisés*, was divided among the fortresses in order to complete their garrisons, and remained until the general disbandment (Appendix Q).

Disbandment of the Army of the North, 7 March 1871

When the Army of the North was disbanded, the minister of war addressed to General Faidherbe the following official letter:

To Monsieur General Faidherbe,

My dear General,
The order of the 7th having called for the disbandment of the active armies and their staffs, I request that you will execute it for the troops under your orders.

At the moment of your laying down your command I beg you to accept all thanks from the government for the aid you have given it in difficult circumstances and for the loyalty of which you have never ceased to give proof.

Please convey to your generals, officers of all ranks, non-commissioned officers and soldiers the thanks of the country for the constancy and efforts which they showed in this campaign, and thanks to which it can be allowed to say that our arms, while not fortunate, have not ceased to be without merit. Their force may have been worn out but not their courage, and the nation relies on them that they will not fail in the new tasks which await them.

This letter will be given out in an army order.

The minister of war
Signed General Le Flô.

[Translator's note – the conclusion is along political lines and hardly concerns military events, and has therefore been omitted.]

Appendices

Appendix A
The remount service of the Army of the North

Between October 1870 and the end of the war in February 1871, the remount service of the Army of the North bought 1,808 team horses, at an average price of 508 francs; 25 mules, at an average of 610 frances; 409 officers' horses, at an average of 721 francs; and 344 men's horses, at an average of 637 francs. The team horses were in most part from Boulonnaise stock. A large number of them came through middlemen from the Ardennes, where it was considered better to sell them rather than see them taken or requisitioned by the enemy.

The riding horses were more difficult to find in a region where they are not raised; it was necessary to take them away even from their owners. In the face of the difficulties which resulted, requisitions were resorted to, but that did not produce good results. The owners whose property was to be requisitioned purchased very mediocre horses, which they presented to the commission, and hid or even sent their good horses to Belgium. Several of them, however, but only a small number, lent theirs to the state for the duration of the war. The total of requisitions was 287 officers' or men's horses, at an average price of 623 francs.

Appendix B
The operations of the intendancy

A question which has caused much noise, brought on many more or less just recriminations and excited spirits, is the fashion in which the troops, and especially the *Mobiles* and *Mobilisés*, were provisioned, armed and equipped during the war.

The Army of the North, like the others (but yet less than the others), had to suffer much. In the first place, it was inevitable during a campaign made during a severe winter and with troops unaccustomed to war. But was this anyone's fault, considering the condition in which we had been placed by the disasters to our regular armies and the loss of our provisions? I do not think so. Everyone knows how difficult it is to improvise an army and to see to its needs in several weeks, even in several months. But that was the task of the intendancy and the administrative corps which depended on it.

Intendants Richard and Montaudon, the former as chief intendant of the Army of the North and the latter as intendant of the 3rd Military Division, went to the limits of their posts, not hesitating to take upon themselves all the responsibility possible in such abnormal circumstances. Here is how the intendancy fulfilled the functions necessary to the forming and training of the Army of the North.

The Army of the North was formed from 1) *Gardes Mobiles* of the three departments of the division, and then from those arriving from neighbouring departments, who were organized in provisional regiments. 2) from officers and men coming from Sedan and Metz, who had escaped from enemy prisons, who were incorporated into the different infantry depots as they came in, or formed the 7th and 11th Dragoon Regiments and a certain number of batteries. 3) last, from *Gardes Nationales mobilisés*, who were organized, clothed and equipped by the civilian authorities.

The military administration had as its first task to note in a regular manner these successive formations, the raising of companies and provisional regiments and to see to the very great needs which resulted. The provisioning, lodging and rest of these men was the first concern, for which the normal resources were very insufficient. Providing for the care of sick men, whether in military or civilian hospitals, was an especial concern. The creation or repair of ambulances which could see to the needs of three headquarters and four infantry divisions. Last, to furnish the units, whose total strength had been raised to 100,000 including garrisons, the items of clothing, equipment and camp necessities they needed.

The major part of the foodstuffs which allowed the Army of the North to be fed had been bought before its formation, since the needs of a siege and, later, the reprovisioning of Paris, had been considered. The urgency of these purchases and their nature did not permit recourse to adjudication. They brought with them an inevitable rise in prices, which considering the importance of the needs was one it was necessary to accept in principle. However, the increases dropped off later owing to the effects of the market, which had been encouraged.

In addition, it was necessary to purchase a large number of items of clothing, equipment and camp necessities, as much as for the Army of the North as to satisfy orders from Nantes and Bordeaux. [Military] manufacturing having been up to this point nearly completely centralized in Paris, the first recourse was to private industry, but it did not prove very efficient. It was necessary to utilize foreign suppliers, in Belgium and England, and in order to speed things up, ministerial authorization was given for the supply of items which differed somewhat from regulation patterns and which were often inferior to them.

Unscrupulous suppliers sometimes evaded the vigilance of the accepting commissions, since these had to inspect a large number of items very quickly, and some of these proved defective on use, for example, shoes whose soles consisted of a piece of cardboard between two layers of leather. When such frauds were detected, the perpetrators were referred to the courts.

Towards the end [of the campaign], the increase in the number of officers allowed the formation of three commissions, and since these were not forced to make quick inspections they proved more efficient. New attempts at fraud could not escape detection, and the suppliers no longer evaded their contractual obligations in the quality of their products. Losses caused by bad manufacturing were nearly insignificant, as far as food, hospitals and camp necessities were concerned. It is difficult to evaluate even in an approximate fashion those of the clothing and small items of equipment. There were numerous complaints about the shoes as well as the jackets and trousers of the *Mobiles*, who were nearly completely outfitted by the civilian authorities.

The rapid deterioration [of items] could in part be ascribed to the difficulties of the campaign, a lack of care in their use; to a certain point they were probably exaggerated by some men, who sought a pretext to conceal their lack of enthusiasm [for the war]. Captures made by the enemy were numerous. First, they consisted of all the supplies which had been assembled for the length of the sieges which it was assumed would occur at Soissons, La Fère, Mézières, Rocroy, the citadel of Amiens and Péronne. Moreover, during the battles of Amiens and Pont-Noyelles, and especially that of Saint-Quentin, and during several other incidents during the war, soldiers had been captured. Others had retreated so quickly so as to be forced to abandon the larger part of their equipment and camp necessities, and several times even their arms.

It is impossible at the present time, before the production of the accounts, to evaluate the importance of losses of this nature.

According to information concerning the expenditures of this war and the experience acquired in it, it appears that 1) it should be necessary in peacetime to have ready all items of clothing, equipment and camp necessities as well as medical items for all the men who enter into a campaign voluntarily, and that these supplies be distributed so as to be delivered to the troops at the places where they have been assembled; 2) at each of these places, which will become fairly numerous, supplies should be provided by local suppliers who are experienced in their manufacture and who in wartime have only to increase the usual methods of production; 3) there should be five or six complete collections of regulation items at each of these locations in order to note them to all manufacturers in order to obtain their understanding of what is required and by that means to obtain entirely regulation products.

Appendix C
The transport service of the Army of the North

Except for several horses and mules which came from Sedan with a detachment of the 3rd Transport Regiment, and which were used to pull ambulances and some regimental wagons as well as to carry packsaddles, litters and *cacolets* made locally, the regular transport did not have much equipment, and each time a movement was made it was necessary to have recourse to the auxiliary transport services, which were requisitioned by the prefects.

The organization of these services, which were reconstituted several times during the course of operations, was as follows: *one- or two-horse wagons* for the baggage of the staff and regimental materials, and which were delivered according to a table ordered by the commanding general; *omnibuses capable of carrying ten people* for large numbers of wounded, one with each ambulance; *two-horse wagons* for stretchers, medical bags, etc., one with each ambulance; *one-horse wagons* for utensils for the food service, one with each division; *two-horse wagons* for a four-day reserve of iron rations and forage, the number differing according to divisional strength; *one-horse wagons* for spare items of minor equipment, four or five at general headquarters; *one-horse wagons* for carrying wounded from the battlefield in the absence of litters and *cacolets*, 10 with general headquarters and 10 for the 2nd Division of 23rd Corps; *omnibus* for money and letter-post items, one per division.

These wagons came with their teams and drivers. After the battle of Saint-Quentin the artillery of the *Garde Nationale mobilisé* sent to the transport a large number of men and horses who had been commandeered by the civilian administration and who were paid from 400 to 500 francs in departmental bonds payable in five years; consequently only wagons and harness were required. The end of hostilities did not permit an evaluation if this mixed system would have produced good results. The requisitioned wagons were paid for by the following schedule, which was approved by the commanding general.

Wagons with horses, harnesses and drivers:
Four-horse wagons with four wheels – 20 francs per day.
Two-horse wagons with four wheels – 12 francs.
One-horse wagons with two wheels – 8 francs.

Three-horse omnibus with four wheels – 20 francs.
Horse with bridle – 5 francs.
Feed for each horse – 2 francs.
Food for each driver – 1 franc, and bread.
Wagons with harnesses only:
Omnibus with eight seats on top – 10 francs per day.
Omnibus with eight seats on top and below – 8 francs.
Two-horse wagon – 4 francs.
One-horse wagon – 3 francs.
Loan of a harness – 25 centimes.

The divisional accountants were ordered to pay these fees every five days upon the presentation of a requisitioning order and a certificate from a transport officer that such measures were necessary. A special office was later created at Lille in order to examine late demands and to pay accounts in arrears; it was in the town hall.

Appendix D
Surrender of the citadel of Amiens

1st Article: The citadel of Amiens, with all warlike material and supplies, will be surrendered to General von Goeben.

2nd Article: All officers, non-commissioned officers and soldiers of the garrison of the citadel will become prisoners of war.

3rd Article: The attendants and storekeepers are to be freed and will retain their private property, except for their arms.

4th Article: The doctor of the ambulance and the medical attendants will be freed according to the Geneva Convention.

5th Article: General von Goeben has considered the unfortunate circumstances in which the garrison has found itself, composed in large part of *Gardes Mobiles* of the region and forced to fire on the buildings. Considering that after three summons to surrender the garrison had borne the fire of the enemy for a day and had only shown the white flag in a gesture of humanity towards the inhabitants of Amiens, and in the face of 72 cannon, placed in batteries to continue the battle, he allows the officers, in honourable recognition, to retain their arms, horses and private property.

The commanding general of the VIII German Army Corps

signed: VON GOEBEN.

Appendix E
Order of the day from General Faidherbe on taking his command

Officers, non-commissioned officers and soldiers,

I have been called to the command of the 22nd Army Corps, and my first duty is to thank the administrators and generals who in several weeks have improvised an army which so honourably proved itself on the 24th, 26th and 27th at Amiens.

I express above all my recognition for General Farre, who commanded you and who, by a skilful retreat in the face of forces double your strength has spared you for the service of the country.

You will take up the campaign again with considerable reinforcements which are being organized every day, and it is up to you to force the enemy to give ground in his turn.

Minister Gambetta has proclaimed that in order to save France he asks of you three things: discipline, strict moral standards and a contempt for death.

I will require that discipline be merciless.

If all cannot attain strict moral standards, I ask for at least dignity and especially temperance. Men under arms for the deliverance of their country have been given too sacred a mission to allow themselves the smallest public disturbance.

As to a contempt for death, I demand it in the name of your salvation. If you do not expose yourself to a glorious death on the battlefield, you will die of misery, you and your families exposed to the merciless yoke of the foreigner. I have no need to add that court martials will deal with cowards, for there are none among you.

5 December 1870
Lieutenant General
Commanding 22nd Army Corps
L. FAIDHERBE

Appendix F
Election of the officers of the Mobiles

The manner in which some officers of *Mobiles* appointed under the Empire behaved themselves caused the commissary for the defence in the region of the North and the commanding general to proceed with the election of officers of the *Garde Mobiles*, according to the new law. This election, made with much speed in the face of the enemy, had good results in some units and bad ones in others.

Several good officers, who were not reelected just because they took the service seriously, were made warrant officers. Soon a number of the newly elected had to be dismissed. They were replaced with regular officers and things went on fairly well from there.

Appendix G
Appointment of the officers of the Army of the North by virtue of the powers granted to the commanding general

Between 18 October 1870 and 28 February 1871 there were appointed for the raising of an army which increased to more than 40,000 men, and in order to replace the grave losses caused by the enemy in four battles and several fights, first by General Bourbaki as commanding general, who was then succeeded by General Faidherbe, both with powers delegated to them by the government of national defense: three lieutenant generals: MM. Paulze d'Ivoy, Lecointe and Farre, all of whose appointments were confirmed by the minister. Two major generals, MM. du Bessol and Derroja, both confirmed by the minister. Sixty-four field officers, 171 captains, 204 lieutenants, 321 sub-lieutenants of all arms.

The losses in regular and auxiliary officers in killed, wounded or missing rose during this period to 487. Two hundred and seventy-nine officers escaped from captivity and were incorporated into the Army of the North, of which they were its best elements.

Appendix H
Report of General von Goeben on the battle of Bapaume
The Prussians denied that they had been beaten at Bapaume; one should not be too astonished at this. It is always easy to be illusory when one's affairs are at state, and in addition not to discourage the army. The document which sheds light on this question is an article in a German newspaper reproduced in *The Daily Telegraph* of 9 January.

> (By submarine telegraph)
> (From our special correspondent)
> Berlin, 8 January.
> General von Göben, Commander of two divisions of the Northern Army, publishes an official report on the engagements of the 2nd and 3rd. He states that too few troops came into action, from the over-slow marches of the forces; and also that the new regiments appeared to be weaker. He demands from the commanders of regiments a list of the officers who fled, that they may be instantly cashiered.

[The translation in French follows, the words "the officers who fled" in italics].

Appendix I
Surrender of Péronne
Signed by Colonel de Hertzberg, Lieutenant-Colonel Gontrand Gonnet, ––– de Bonnault, commander of the artillery, and Major Cadot, the plenipotentiaries of Lieutenant General Baron von Barnekow and Major Garnier, commandant of the fortress of Péronne.

It is agreed that:

1st Article. The garrison of Péronne under Major Garnier, commandant of the fortress, is to be prisoner of war. The *Garde Nationale Sédentaire* is not included in this article.

2nd Article. The fortress and town of Péronne, with all warlike material, the majority of the supplies of all sorts and all state property will be surrendered to the Prussian force commanded by Lieutenant General Baron von Barnekow in the state in which it is when this convention is signed. At 11 a.m. tomorrow, 10 January, artillery and engineer officers with several non-commissioned officers will be admitted into the fortress in order to occupy the powder and ammunition magazines.

3rd Article. All arms, artillery equipment, horses, military chests, army equipment, ammunition, etc., will remain in Péronne in the hands of military commissions appointed by the commandant in order to be turned over to Prussian commissions. At 1 p.m. the troops, ordered by corps and with military order, will be conducted onto the Paris road, their left adjoining the works and their right towards Etrepigny, where they will lay down their arms. The officers will be allowed to return freely to the town, under condition of giving their word of honour not to leave it without an order from the Prussian commandant. The troops will be therefore led by their non-commissioned officers. The soldiers will keep their packs, belongings and camp equipment, tents, blankets and mess tins.

4th Article. Field and subaltern officers and military officials with officer's rank who give their word of honour in writing not to bear arms against Germany and not to act against her interests until the end of the present war will not be made prisoners of war. The officers and officials who accept this condition will retain their arms and personal property. They may leave Péronne when they wish, having first obtained Prussian permission.

The officers who are prisoners of war will take their swords or sabres as well as their private property and will retain their servants. They will leave on a day to be fixed by the Prussian commandant. Military doctors will remain behind to take care of the wounded and sick and will be treated according to the Geneva Convention, as will the hospital personnel.

5th Article. No inhabitant of the town, private or public, is to be disturbed or prosecuted by the Prussian authorities for the actions they took in the war. Because of the energetic resistance of Péronne, and also considering its poor situation and the destruction caused by the bombardment, it will be exempted from all requisitioning of food and money. The inhabitants will not be required to feed German soldiers until the majority of the supplies found in the public magazines has been exhausted. This condition will not apply to the day of entry [of the Prussian troops].

6th Article. The arms of the *Garde Nationale Sédentaire* will be deposited at the town hall and will come under Prussian control. Civilian weapons will be deposited there also but will remain the property of their owners.

7th Article. Any article about which there are doubts will be interpreted in favour of the French army.

8th Article. At noon on 10 January the gates of Saint-Nicolas and Britanny will be opened for the entry of Prussian troops. At the same time the following works, Couronne de Bretagne and Couronne de Paris, will be evacuated by their French garrison.
Cartigny, 9 January 1871, 11 p.m.
Signed von Hertzberg,
Colonel.

Appendix J
Recapture of Saint-Quentin, 15 January 1871
In conformity to the orders of the commanding general, Colonel Isnard, commander of the brigade detached to the east, had marched from Cambrai on 14 January towards Saint-Quentin, which was occupied by the troops of the Prince of Saxony. He sent Colonel de

Vintmille with two battalions of *Mobiles* through Bohain and Fresnoy-le-Grand, passing through Masnières and Bellicourt with the rest of his troops.

At Bonavy he encountered a Prussian detachment of 500 infantrymen, two squadrons and two cannon, and it fell back towards Le Catelet, where there was a minor advance-guard action. He was attacked at Bellicourt and Noroy, but pushed the enemy back after dismounting one of their guns. The Prussians retired into Saint-Quentin.

Arriving at daybreak the following day before Saint-Quentin, Colonel Isnard took post with his brigade 200 metres from the Saint-Jean suburb. He advanced the battalion of the 24th Line Infantry, supported by the skirmishers of the Zouaves of the North, and placed his two field pieces and four mountain guns in order to reply to the Prussian artillery at the mill of Rocourt. The skirmishers, followed by the main body of the troops, entered the suburb and then the city, which the Prussians evacuated without strong resistance.

At the battle of Bellicourt eight of our men were wounded, and at the capture of Saint-Quentin one dead and six wounded. The enemy left 40 prisoners in our hands at Saint-Quentin, forage, eight officers' baggage wagons, food and cigars, 25 cavalry horses and a field smithy.

Appendix K
History of a battery of Mobiles

It is necessary here to relate the history of the Dupuich *Mobile* battery in order to demonstrate that it is not absurd to believe that units capable of great deeds can be drawn from the ranks of the *Mobiles* and *Mobilisés*, providing they are bravely led.

In September 1870 a *Mobile* battery was formed at Arras with horses and several drivers from the engineer regiment in garrison there. The men of this battery were young inhabitants of Arras and Boulogne. Initially its officers were Lieutenants Belvallette from Boulogne and Delalé from Arras. The engineers having been obliged to reclaim their horses, the civilian authorities of the department provided their replacements. M. Dupuich was then named captain of the battery, M. Delattre from Calais its first lieutenant, and M. Garet its veterinary. *This battery had not fired a shot, not even a blank one, nor had it performed any artillery manoeuvres* before it was incorporated on 17 December into the 23rd Corps of the Army of the North. For its initiation to action it took post on 23 December during the battle of Pont-Noyelles facing a group of Prussian batteries, which had just silenced an excellent 12-pounder naval battery in the same spot.

The *Mobile* battery, despite having had in a very short time three axles and a caisson broken and several horses killed, hesitated only a moment. It bravely fired shells towards an advancing Prussian column. Having repulsed it, the battery was placed in another position, where it remained until the end of the battle.

Military writers will argue until they are blind about whether it takes three, four or five years to form a gunner, if it is necessary for a man to have been at the *École polytechnique* to become a battery officer, and yet here are civilians who underwent their baptism of fire in the face of the so much vaunted Prussian artillery of this war and fought with honour. A veteran formation from its first shot, the battery later took the most active part over the two days of Bapaume, where it fired 600 rounds the first day and 420 the second, and then in the fight at Vermand, where it was practically alone and where it fired 900 rounds, halting the enemy with canister fire. Last, it was at Saint-Quentin, where it fired 600 rounds and helped stop an enemy outflanking movement on our right wing.

In these two latter battles it was commanded by Captain Belvallette. On 10 January Captain Dupuich, who was at some distance from the column during the march from Bapaume to Saint-Quentin, was captured by a party of Prussian hussars after killing a trooper with his revolver. During its month of fighting the battery of the *Mobiles* of Pas-du-Calais had fired 2,165 rounds, had 30 non-commissioned officers or soldiers killed or wounded and 50 horses put out of action. The only non-*Mobile* troops were part of the drivers and several naval gun layers.

Appendix L
The new shells of General de Beaulieu

At the battle of Saint-Quentin there was fired for the first time the new shrapnel round designed by General Treuille de Beaulieu, and which had been adopted by the government of national defence on 17 December 1870.

Two batteries, those of Captains Bocquillon and Halphen, fired these new rounds, which weighed about 5 kilograms. They contained an average of 46 pieces or balls. The increased weight of the new round necessitated several changes to the method of firing. The usual wartime powder charge was increased by 50 grams to 600 grams. This increase, which had to be limited because of the great shock to the carriage, was insufficient to redress the decrease in range which resulted by the increase in weight of the round. The difference was made up by increasing elevation, and it was recognized as necessary with the new rounds to fire 100 metres longer than the actual range.

These things were certainly inconveniences, but they were largely compensated for by the advantages of the new round. It is to be understood that all these new rounds were, like the older ones, fitted with percussion fuses.

The batteries which fired these new rounds did so at ranges of 2,500 and 2,000 metres, with remarkable accuracy and a considerable material and moral effect. In hitting the ground, the shell burst into fragments which covered the ground from 200 to 300 metres from the point of impact. This result, whose effect was verified by direct observation, was moreover confirmed by the great efforts of the enemy artillery to concentrate their fire on the batteries armed with this new shell, as a result ignoring to some extent the larger-calibre batteries near to them. The effects of this shell on infantry columns produced disorder and rout. Against batteries this shellfire produced an immediate slackening of enemy fire.

Orders having been given for as complete an observation as possible, and the written and verbal reports from the captains commanding were precise and in agreement. They were unanimous in testifying to the remarkable effect of these new shells.

All civilians, sick, prisoners and escapees who came from the places held by the 1st Prussian Army are in agreement in stating that the Prussians held the artillery of the Army of the North in high regard. "Your artillery is remarkable," they said, "and the fire of your mitrailleuses did us much injury; you have not been so served before." An officer of the staff of General Lecointe, Baron de Cantillon, was sent on a mission to the Prussian staff, reported that he had been told "The artillery of the Army of the North is very good, but you are not *truthful*. You had a battery of mitrailleuses at Saint-Quentin and did not admit it."

During a mission which Colonel Charon undertook to Paris after the armistice by order of the commanding general, he himself had the opportunity at Amiens to meet the staff of General von Goeben, the commander of the 1st Army, and he heard similar expressions from the Prussian officers who had been present [at the battle]. All praised the excellent shooting of the Army of the North and were astonished to encounter mitrailleuses once more. However, the Army of the North never had mitrailleuses, and perhaps the new shrapnel round led our enemies to believe the contrary. Thus was established the position of the new rounds, which were of great power, and their initial effect has been to double the value of our 4-pounder rifled cannon, which according to Colonel Charon, when well directed and at a useful range remains an excellent arm which can traverse all sorts of ground. Its lack of range has been criticized; this criticism has not as much value as has been thought. Colonel Charon of the artillery believes that a field gun with a range of 6,000 metres would be ineffective if sited 7,000 metres from enemy batteries.

Appendix M
The medical service of the Army of the North

The medical establishment of the Army of the North was directed by *Médécin-Inspecteur* Lavrean, whose merit and devotion to duty are well known. He did all that was possible in circumstances made very difficult by the rigour of the season and the speed of the army's movements. What follows is taken from his report made to the commanding general.

The death rate following considerable surgical operations was 67 out of 100. That following an operation on the lower limbs was nearly 74 out of 100, and of the upper limbs 59 out of 100. This high death rate cannot be accounted for by only one reason, the gathering together of a large number of wounded and infection where they lay, for it varied only slightly from one town to the next, in the hospitals and ambulances. It is not possible to attribute a sole condition to the deplorably high death rate, which also implies that the methods of treatment were at fault and that war is unfeeling. By doing so everything which had a deathly influence is ignored; the excessive fatigues of the campaign in an extremely rigorous winter, and last the depression caused by the cold and the lack of energy of the men when their willpower could not stand up.[1] All these factors came together to increase the total of our dead and the lengthening of our misfortunes.

It is now proper to recognize the debt owed to the country by the aid from the towns, private charity and the Red Cross Society. The Army of the North had large hospitals and ambulances in its rear, and whose overall capacity ranged from 6,000 to 12,000 beds. The inhabitants generally were very eager to receive the wounded and convalescents. In the towns, where all competed in charity and sympathy in a common bereavement, there was only the wish to do them well.

There were doubtless abuses: in several cases, egotism assumed the mask of devotion to duty. The Red Cross flag was flown, several stragglers from the battlefield were taken in in order to obtain the price paid for lodging soldiers, but overall individual weaknesses did not diminish the greatness of the patriotism and generosity of the towns of Saint-Quentin, Arras, Douai, Cambrai, Corbie, Avesne, Lille and the majority of the towns and villages occupied by our troops. The persons who showed themselves devoted and charitable would make a list as long as it is honourable to the country. At its head were M. Leopold Lebé of Saint-Quentin, the Archbishop of Cambrai, the Bishop of Arras, M.

---

1 During the rapid marches and days of battle it was not often impossible for the men to cook, and this lack of sufficient food gave the men anemia and those who were wounded became listless. The sausages of the Prussians had a great effect in many cases. When our men could not cook, they threw away their meat, which they could not eat raw, and subsisted only on bread.

Galle, estate official at Corbie, the sisters of the hospital in the same town, the directors of the *Société de Secours* of Douai, MM. Léonard Danel, August Longhaye and Arnoux of Lille. The members of the university competed in zeal with the clergy and it would be an act of ingratitude to omit to mention among them the principal of the college of Arras.

A justified tribute is due to the Belgian Red Cross Society, which at Haussoy, Franvillers and Vermand took great care for the needs of our wounded, when the ambulances were ordered to follow the army in its movements on Albert, Bapaume and Saint-Quentin. The English societies and the London Society, which was represented at Lille by Baron de Saint-Didier, lavished on our wounded men all that an inexhaustible charity could find, and created for itself goodwill and a testimony of the sympathy which is the aim of generous hearts of all nations.

Several clergymen, principally Dominicans, followed the army as chaplains. One of them, Father Mercier, was wounded four times at the battle of Amiens, where he displayed remarkable courage.

Appendix N
Order of the day from the commanding general after the battle of Saint-Quentin
After the battle of Saint-Quentin, in order to lessen the depression which ran through an army forced to retreat after having suffered much, the commanding general found it necessary to address to it the following order of the day:

Douai, 21 January.

Soldiers!
It is a pressing necessity for your general to render you justice before your fellow citizens. You can be proud of yourselves, and you have well merited your country.

You have suffered what those who have not seen it can never imagine, and there is no-one to blame for this suffering; circumstances alone caused it.

In less than a month you have fought three battles and several actions with an enemy which all Europe fears. You have held him; you have seen him fall back many times before you, you have proved that he is not invincible and that the defeat of France was no more than an incident caused by the ineptitude of an absolute government.

The Prussians have found in young, badly clothed soldiers and in the *Gardes Nationales* adversaries who can beat them. Who cares if they gather up stragglers and boast of it in their bulletins! These famous takers of guns have not touched one of your batteries.

Honour to you!
Several days of rest, and those who have sworn the ruin of France will find us right back against them.

Appendix O
Examples of orders of the day of the Prussian army
In a house which had been occupied by a German officer there were found at the base of the chimney, in the middle of the ashes, partly burned papers, among which was almost an entire series of orders of the day of the Prussian army.

These documents show much order, method and precision; the smallest details are set out and the means of transmission completely set out; all show the admirable organization of the Prussian army and its staff. In addition, they demonstrate the extreme ease by which a brigade or a division is transferred to another corps and in the formation of detachments, without encountering the obstacles placed in the way of such movements by personal rivalries.

I do not believe it possible to do more in the way of military organization. An excellent spirit appears to have animated everyone. In this army, from the ordinary soldier to the general, and I would even say to the sovereign, there is a great confidence and even a great mutual esteem.

However, I remain convinced in the superiority of the French soldier of the Army of the North over the German soldier. If the latter is larger, stronger and more disciplined, the French soldier, free since the revolution, has a greater personal valour. A soldier who is beaten, whipped and slapped as the Prussian is by his leaders cannot come up to one who is not submitted to this debasing discipline.

There follow extracts from these orders of the day. Several will certainly have been found characteristic.

[The first two orders give the German versions, then the French translations; the remainder are in French only]

Rouen, 8 December 1870.
Order of the day
2. His Majesty the King has ordered that there will be an increase to two pairs of socks per man. In executing this order, the minister of war has ordered a sufficient quantity that I, VII and VIII corps will receive 20,000 pair, the Lenden Division 6,000 and the 3rd Cavalry Division 2,500. The corps or divisions which require more can obtain them through requisitions, the preference being to requisitions in territory as yet unoccupied. The despatch of the socks will be performed by the general inspection of the rear areas.

signed von Manteuffel.

Divisional order
Having been transferred by His Majesty's order to another corps, I cannot leave the division without thanking the officers and soldiers for their services and for the good will which they have shown on every occasion.
I add my best wishes for the New Year, with the hope that we will soon return home.
2. Giving out of orders tonight at 9.
3. Password: *Famine.* Countersign: *Martin.*

Versailles, 12 December 1870
M. A. C. O. K. K.
Given the high cost of living in France, we increase to 30 thalers per month the pay of first lieutenants, second lieutenants and doctors with equivalent ranks, as well as the higher officials of the German Army of the North.

Order of 22 December
On receipt there will be sent the sections 8 and 13 of the staff maps at a scale of 1: 80 000, and for the section 8 (for Lille), a general map at 1: 120 000. One example will be given to each head of a brigade, one to each regimental staff, two to each battalion and squadron and four to the artillery.

   Each cavalry and infantry brigade will receive small road maps.
   The infantry brigade will receive six examples of a road map.

Amiens, 30 December 1870.
It is brought to the attention of the army that His Excellency the minister of war Roon will celebrate the anniversary of his 50th year of military service on 9 January 1871.

Amiens, 1 January 1871.
A unit commander has learned that French officers have said that Prussian officers can be easily recognized by their rubber raincoats and that as a result they are pointed out as an ideal target for their infantry.

Brigade order
Tomorrow at noon will be handed in the state of the men of the several regiments who have left for Amiens with unsound feet.

Combles, 2 January 1871, 9 P.M.
Corps order
The enemy has today taken the offensive towards Bapaume and Bucquoy. The Kummer Division has halted the attack directed on it and is near Bapaume. The cavalry division is at Miraumont. I order for tomorrow that:
1. Lieutenant General von Kummer will hold the neighbourhood of Bapaume.
2. The 3rd Cavalry Division will take the offensive and move against the flank and the rear of the enemy.
3. Prince Albrecht will be at 9 A.M. near Bertincourt with three battalions, two batteries, the 9th Hussars, the 2nd Lancer Guards and a horse battery. A squadron of the Hussar Guards is to remain at La Chelle.
4. A rifle battalion and two horse batteries will be at Translois by 9 A.M.
5. Lieutenant General von Barnekow will set on their march the four batteries of the 2nd Division, accompanied by three battalions, in such a manner that they will be near Sailly-Sailssel (between Bapaume and Péronne) by 9 A.M. They are to be commanded by a capable staff officer who has been placed at my disposal....
During the night each division and detachment will send out patrols towards the enemy.

                                                                        von Goeben

Dompierre, 4 January 1871.
Headquarters
The flying columns and long-range patrols do not need to return to their units the same day. On the contrary, they are recommended to eat in one place and sleep in

another, and to come back after having eaten in a third place, all the time sending back numerous reports.

von Goeben

Dompierre, 5 January 1871.
Headquarters
It has been reported that there has been found on a French non-commissioned officer taken prisoner or in the uniform of a dead man a state for a Franco-Belgian legion. Units will inquire about it and report the results to me up to 10 P.M....

Fusilier Schneider of the 7th Company of the 69th Regiment, who had remained in the rear at Béhencourt on the 24th with a wounded man, has not reappeared. His fate is to be looked into and the results communicated to me up to 10 P.M.

von Goeben

Amiens, 6 January 1871
1. Unit commanders are advised that it is now possible to use the railway between Rheims, Laon and La Fère to bring up clothing for the troops.
2. Despite repeated orders, requisitions have again been made without authorization in Amiens and its suburbs. Requisitions without the approval of the commanding general or the intendancy are once more forbidden. Any contraventions will be punished.

von Manteuffel

6 January 1871.
Brigade order
I forbid in the strongest fashion all requisitioning by soldiers. Only the commander has the right to requisition, through the mayors.

7 January 1871.
Order of the day – headquarters
The 56 French officers included on the following list have broken their parole of honour and have escaped from the place assigned to them. If they are retaken, they are to be immediately conducted to the commanding general of the 1st Army.[2]

Then follows the note: The two last men have been taken.

Dompierre, 7 January 1871.
On 31 December at Combles a white mare, harnessed to a baggage wagon, was taken from the quarters of General von Manteuffel. It must be found and returned to its owner, or if this is not possible he is to be given a bill.

The results are to be sent in on the 14th.

---

2   Note by the author that of the 56 men, one was from the staff of Marshal Bazaine, three from the artillery, one from the *chasseurs à pied*, one from the *infanterie de marine*, three from the cavalry, one from the *Garde Mobile*, two from the Imperial Guard and 40 from the infantry.

Belloy, 8 January, 11 p.m.
Tomorrow at noon the intendancy will deliver to Harbonnières on receiving the receipts the furs for the use of sentries; they must be taken especial care of. Each infantry battalion, except the 2nd of the 81st, will receive eight furs; each cavalry regiment, including the two regiments of the Guards cavalry, 50 furs.

Belloy, 8 January.
The commanding general of VII Corps has informed us that he has had to severely punish soldiers who took things from shops without paying. The discipline and good behaviour of the troops is to be strictly attended to by unit commanders.

Dompierre, 9 January.
Péronne has fallen. Today at 2 p.m. our troops entered and took possession of the fortress. More than 5,000 prisoners, about 40 cannon and a great quantity of supplies have fallen into our hands.

von Goeben

Amiens, 10 January 1871.
1. General von Manteuffel having been called to other duties by higher order, I take provisional command of the 1st Army.
2. The unit commanders will announce through the mayors of all towns occupied by our troops that it is forbidden to ring bells for any purpose other than religion. The ringing of bells is therefore only to be allowed by the church authorities, who will be held personally responsible if by ringing bells harm is done to our troops in any way.
3. The woollen shirts and socks which have been or will be distributed to the soldiers during the course of the campaign will remain their property. Their replacement will only be by requisitioning and not from Germany. Their state is to be inscribed in the account books.

von Goeben

Dompierre, 10 January, 10:30 p.m.
Order for VIII Corps
The 16th Infantry Division will change its position as soon as General von Barnekow judges it to be possible, occupying the right bank of the Somme in such a fashion as to observe the enemy and maintain communications with Saint-Quentin.
Péronne must be put in a state of defence at all costs. The prisoners of war will be sent to La Fère under the escort of two companies and a squadron.
If the enemy advances, the commanding general is to be notified at the same time as the brigades closest to them.

von Goeben

Dompierre, 12 January 1871.
Corps order
The 16th Infantry Division will order an engineer officer to reconnoitre the length of the Somme between Péronne and Bray and report on the state of the locks.

Amiens, 14 January 1871.
Colonel von Wittich has this night pushed the enemy back towards Bapaume and bombarded the town, which he has burned, and retired with but a weak pursuit.[3]

14 January 1871.
Order for the 16th Division
The detachment of Colonel von Wittich, which advanced yesterday up to Bapaume, found this town and the villages on the Albert road strongly occupied by the enemy. After having alarmed them and bombarded Bapaume, he returned, pursued only weakly, without having suffered loss.

von Barnekow.

Amiens, 13 January 1871.
Order of the day
By an order of the 6th to the corps, His Majesty has been graciously pleased to confer the Iron Cross 1st Class on the following officers and soldiers: Colonel von Bock, commanding the 22nd Brigade; Major Busch of the general staff of VIII Corps; Colonel von Kamecke, commanding the 8th Artillery Brigade; Sergeant Harting of the 8th Rhenish Field Artillery Regiment; Major Sax of the 70th Regiment; Captain Litski of the 28th Regiment; Colonel von Wittich of the 9th Hussars; Colonel von Rosenzweig of the 28th.

von Goeben

Order of the day. Headquarters at Amiens, 15 January 1871.
In order to control the correspondence along the relay line Amiens-Villers-Bretonneux-Proyard-Estrée-Péronne, proper billets will be issued through the commanders. These billets, delivered by the commanding general, will be reported to his staff the first time it is necessary to use them.
Commanders of detachments charged with relaying orders are to take all measures to ensure that the service is carried on with more speed than in the past. In this regard they must have horses always saddled, send them off without delay, and order the troopers to make two miles an hour even if it is snowing and icy. If these precautions are followed, a letter will take but 10 hours, for example, to go between Amiens and Péronne.
The 3rd Reserve Division (minus the Strantz Cavalry Brigade) will receive tomorrow examples of 1: 80 000 maps for the sections on Amiens and Arras, 26 of the former and 13 of the latter. A receipt is to be sent.
von Goeben

15 January 1871.
Order for the 16th Division

---

3 This news was completely false and was contradicted by the following order, which is still exaggerated. The main headquarters of the French army was this day at Bapaume, and no one noticed that it had been bombarded by the hussar Colonel von Wittich. A few minutes before noon a detachment appeared two to three kilometres from Bapaume, but it retreated more speedily than it came up, after having fired several shells which did not reach the town.

The men will not carry their packs but are to take along their mess tins and a complete load of cartridges. The packs will be transported in wagons and sent to the rear.

Barnekow

Amiens, 16 January 1871

There are at Péronne 160 chassepots taken from the enemy. Detachments which wish to have a certain number of them can receive them from the commandant of Péronne, giving a receipt.

von Goeben

Orders for the corps. Nesle, 17 January 1871, 11 p.m.

According to reports received, the enemy has concentrated considerable forces at Saint-Quentin and has pushed outposts in the direction of Péronne and Ham. I order that tomorrow:

1. The 15th Infantry Division will march at 8 a.m. through Tertry towards Ervillers and the neighbourhood. At daybreak it is to send patrols along this route and in the direction of Vermand.
2. The detachment of Lieutenant General Count von den Groeben will march on Vermand. When it arrives at the outskirts it will place itself under the command of Lieutenant General von Kummer, who is to reconnoitre the enemy position.
3. The 16th Infantry Division will march at 8 a.m. on Jussy, from where it is to send detachments towards Saint-Quentin to discover if the enemy is there or in which direction he is marching. Lieutenant General Count Lippe is asked to march on Vendeuil and Moy.

The 3rd Reserve Division will leave at 8 a.m. for Ham and at daybreak is to send patrols towards Saint-Quentin. An officer will be at my headquarters at 8 a.m.

5. The artillery of VIII Corps will move at 10 a.m. towards Ugny and Quivières and their vicinity.
6. The transport....
7. I will leave at 9 a.m. for Ham, to where the daily reports are to be sent.

von Goeben

NB: the 3rd Reserve Division is no longer under the command of the 16th Infantry Division but under that of the commanding general of VIII Corps.

Order at 9 p.m.

Order for the 16th Infantry Division 17 January 1871

Combles, Rancourt and Bouchavesne have been occupied by the enemy. The *infanterie de marine* is at Bellenglise. At Saint-Quentin there are about 4,000 men. The division of Count Lippe has occupied Roupy. It appears that the enemy has fallen back from the vicinity of Albert and has gone along the Cambrai road to Saint-Quentin. In order to confirm this, I order that:

1. A reconnaissance force, led by Lieutenant Colonel Reineck, with two battalions, four guns and two squadrons will move from Tincourt towards Hurlu and Fins.
2. Patrols will be strengthened by the detachments at Roisel and Vermand.
3. A battalion and a battery will tomorrow at 10 a.m. move on Tincourt and Boudy.

4. The Fusilier Battalion of the 70th Regiment will concentrate tomorrow at 10 a.m. at Mons-en-Chausée, with the 5th heavy battery.
5. Tomorrow at 10 a.m. the Fusilier Battalion of the 29th Regiment will post two companies at each of the Somme bridges at Brie and Saint-Christ.
6. In order to meet all eventualities, the baggage, except that of the garrison of Péronne, will be assembled tomorrow at 9 a.m. That of the 31st Infantry Brigade will be at Barleux, that of the 32nd Infantry Brigade and the reserve brigade at Villers-Carbonnel, that of the advance guard and 3rd Reserve Division at Flancourt, that of the main body of the infantry and the 2nd Lancer Guards Regiment at Marchelpot. The detachments which are to march will leave their baggage in their quarters and loaded on vehicles as much as possible. These vehicles will be sent to the baggage park if needed. The mess tins and cartridges are to be carried by the men.
7. All information which comes in which could be of use for the advance of the Reineck detachment is to be sent without delay in its direction.
8. The 3rd Reserve Division of His Royal Highness Prince Albrecht is in part to guard and defend the bridges and passages re-established at Feullière and Hem. The troops of the 31st Infantry Brigade quartered on the left bank of the Somme (1st Battalion 29th and 5th heavy battery at Biaches below Péronne) will take part in the movement, under the command of Lieutenant Colonel von Hymmen. The bridges are to be totally destroyed if the enemy advances with superior numbers. The 3rd Reserve Division is also to hold itself in readiness to occupy the defiles above Péronne in case the troops on the right bank are obliged to evacuate it.

Barnekow.

Order for the 3rd Reserve Division
18 January 1871, 12:45 A.M.
1. The advance guard, with the exception of the 1st Battalion 81st Regiment, will at 8 A.M. move from Mesnil Saint-Nicaise to Ham by way of Rouy-le-Petit, Eppeville and Voyennes. At daybreak it is to send reconnaissances towards Saint-Quentin.
2. At 9:30 A.M. the main body of the infantry, including the 1st Battalion 81st, the 2nd Lancer Guards and the 1st Squadron of the Hussar Guards Regiment, will assemble to the north of Hombleux in the position indicated.
3. At the same place at 9:30 the advance guard will assemble, and at 10 the brigade.
4. The wagon park and the baggage will leave tomorrow for Nesle.
5. I will be at the head of the main body of the infantry.

Albrecht, Prince of Prussia.

Doubts have arisen on the subject of the auxiliary stretcher-bearers from the troops, who always wear the white armband with a red cross. In order not to give the enemy any pretext for acts of violence, I order that these men will not wear the armband while they are considered as combatants; their armbands will be assembled and stowed in the vehicles of the units. During major actions, when it becomes necessary to reinforce the medical detachments, the armband will be given to these men, who naturally will then leave off their arms and their pouches.

Army order
Ham, 18 January 1871, 10 P.M.
The 15th Infantry Division and the detachment of General Count Groeben have in a victorious battle repulsed the enemy forces opposed to them and taken a gun, but without having pursued the enemy vigorously enough nor to have arrived at the positions assigned to them. The victory must be completed on the morrow.

General von Kummer will move tomorrow morning at 8 all the troops under his orders, including all the corps artillery, along the roads of Vermand and Étreillers and will march vigorously on Saint-Quentin.

The troops under General von Kummer are sufficient in number to fight with success the entire French Army of the North. They are to fall on all those before them, encircle them and take Saint-Quentin. In order to do so, General Count Groeben is to extend his forces to the left up to the road from Cambrai to Saint-Quentin.

The division of Count Lippe, with the attached 16th Infantry Brigade, will support this movement. It is to arrive at Tergnier tomorrow morning, and will at the same time move vigorously towards the road from La Fère to Saint-Quentin, turning the enemy right as much as possible.

With the forces assembled under my command and with our superior artillery, it only needs to advance with energy and to throw back all that the enemy can oppose to us.

The reserve under Colonel von Bocking will tomorrow morning march from Ham towards Saint-Quentin. To it will be joined a squadron of the 9th Hussar Regiment, which it will pick up at Ham, and the 2nd Squadron of the Lancer Guards, which is to arrive at Ham around 9 A.M. and will report to Colonel von Bocking.

I will be with the reserve at the beginning of the action, and reports are to be sent to me there. It is probable that I shall subsequently rejoin the Kummer Division.

If the enemy does not wait for our assault, the pursuit is to be carried on with the greatest energy and with the greatest effort. Experience teaches us that when faced by troops so badly organized, a battle does not give the greatest results but rather its disorganizing effects, and we should exploit this.

von Goeben.

Army order
19 January 1871
The French Army of the North has been completely beaten; Saint-Quentin has been occupied by the divisions of General Barnekow and His Royal Highness Prince Albrecht. Two cannon have been taken in the course of the fight. More than 4,000 prisoners have been taken.

I congratulate the troops whom I have the honour to command. The fruits of our victory must now be gathered. We have fought today; tomorrow we must advance in order to achieve the rout of the enemy. He *appears* to have retired partly on Cambrai and partly on Guise.[4] *He must be fallen on* before he can move into the shelter of the line of the fortresses.

In order to do so, I make it a rule that the troops must march about five miles per day (about 10 kilometric miles). Wherever possible the infantry will transport

---

4 A mistake. No French unit was directed towards Guise.

its packs in wagons. General von Kummer will march on Cambrai, while General von Barnekow, with the 16th Infantry Division, the division of Prince Albrecht and the Bocking detachment, which was today placed under his command, will march through Sequehart on Clary and Caudry. The division of Count Lippe will move on Bohain and Cateau-Cambrésis.

I will move to Cadelet for the time being. I will be there by noon and will there receive the reports of the generals named above.

von Goeben.

Order of the day
Caudry, 21 January 1871
His Majesty the King has been graciously pleased to confer on Lieutenant General Barnekow and Lieutenant General von Kummer the Order of the *Pour le Mérite* with oak leaves.

von Goeben

Caudry, 21 January 1871
Lieutenant General Gebauer is appointed commandant of Péronne.

The reports on our losses (mentioning officers by name) in the battles at Saint-Quentin are to be sent tomorrow at 7 p.m. to the commanding general, who is in Saint-Quentin.

von Goeben.

Army order
Headquarters Caudry, 21 January
1. Tomorrow General von Kummer, with the 15th Division and that portion of the corps artillery attached to him, will move into the region of Achiet, Bapaume, Beugny and Beaumetz and will send detachments to observe towards Cambrai and Arras.
2. General von Kummer will command units of all arms in his district. In the unlikely event that *he is pressured by the enemy* he will retreat on Arras.
3. General Count Groeben will remain before Cambrai in the region of Marcoing, Masnières and Crevecœur. He is to keep up communications with Generals von Kummer and von Barnekow and is to reconnoitre the enemy.

If the enemy pressures him he is to retire on Péronne.

von Goeben.

16th Infantry Division
Prémont, 22 January 1871
I was struck today by the large number of non-regulation wagons of all sorts. I order that the wagon park be reduced to the lowest size. I have already said that the baggage will be placed behind the columns of march and therefore away from the enemy. When a retreat is ordered, it therefore means that the baggage is to be sent on ahead, followed by the troops.

von Barnekow.

Corps order
Lieutenant General von Barnekow,
I request Your Excellency to raise contributions today and tomorrow in the districts occupied by your troops. I assign you the districts of Clary, Catelet, Solesmes and Carnières, the latter two as much as possible. A rule of 25 francs a head is to be established, but it will not always be possible to raise such a high rate.

It is necessary to send to the rear and to take all that can be seized in flour. The horses which we have lost will have to replaced and to exchange those which have become unfit for service. It is also useful to bring off many cattle. But entirely regulation requisitioning bonds are to be given for everything, accompanied with receipts which state their value. The money is to be sent to the intendancy of VIII Corps.

Caudry, 22 January 1871.

von Goeben.

Order for the 3rd Reserve Division
Maretz, 23 January 1871, 10:30 a.m.
1. The boots which have followed the provisions column belong to the 81st and are to be distributed to the men today.
2. When the boots have been delivered by the army intendancy, if one unit finds itself with a surplus and another still lacks some, a readjustment will be made by the proper authorities and in the last case by Colonel von Goeben and Major von Schweinchen....

I must remark again that the food of the men and horses must above all be furnished by the districts in which they are quartered, especially meat, flour and bread. When these items cannot be furnished by the inhabitants, the districts are to be forced to bake bread.

Albrecht, Prince of Prussia.

Brigade order. 24 January 1871.
The three inhabitants of Péronne who have been taken as hostages by the Lancer Guards and the report of Major von Kapphengst on this subject will be sent to the commanding general in Saint-Quentin by the 1st Battalion 81st. The hostages will be placed in a wagon.

Order of the day. Headquarters Amiens, 28 January 1871.
His Majesty has been graciously pleased to order that a summary report is to be made to him in person and as soon as possible on each action of some importance or when a brigade particularly distinguishes itself. This report is to be made by the commanding officer in the action. He will describe it and its result.

Order of the day. Amiens, 29 January 1871.
I have been told by Count Moltke in a letter of the 23rd that he has signed an armistice which will commence at noon on 31 January. The cessation of hostilities will be immediately acceded to on the basis of the status quo if the enemy requests it.

von Goeben.

Divisional order
Headquarters Deniécourt, 29 January 1871.
9 p.m.
At 2 tomorrow afternoon there will be a meeting of the commission for the purchase of horses for the 2nd Lancer Guards Regiment in front of the quarters of Captain von Below. Those officers who wish to sell riding horses are requested to send them to Chaulnes at the hour indicated, giving their price.

Albrecht, Prince of Prussia.

Army order
Amiens, 30 January 1871.
Under the conditions of the armistice, the departments of Pas-du-Calais and Nord are exempted from German occupation, and it has been agreed that the outposts will remain at least 10 kilometres from the demarcation line. In consequence, the advance ordered for tomorrow will be partly halted, and some places occupied by us are to be evacuated. However, these operations will only take place when General Faidherbe has evacuated Abbeville and the entire department of the Somme. In any case, from noon tomorrow, the 31st, all encounters with the enemy are to be avoided, and all enemy detachments are to be met by parliamentaries, who will inform them that negotiations are proceeding with Faidherbe.

von Goeben.

Appendix P
Report of General Faidherbe on the impossibility of continuing the war in the Nord, at the armistice

This measure was taken by the government in the wake of the report below which was sent by the commanding general of the Army of the North, in answer to the question which was addressed to him during the armistice: "Can the war be continued?" General Faidherbe answered:

Minister,
The military forces of the departments of Nord and Pas-du-Calais consist of:
1. A regular army (22nd and 23rd corps), consisting at this time of about 25,000 men, a third of whom are regulars, a third mobiles and a third *mobilisés*, and which possesses 16 good field batteries.
2. The garrisons of 15 fortresses, consisting of *mobilisés*, infantry and artillery and about 55,000 men.[5]
These fortresses will require 80,000 men in order to make a strong defence.
If war restarts after the expiration of the armistice, it must be said that the Prussians will send from 80,000 to 100,000 men against the north, with strong siege trains available at Paris. Faced with such forces, the Army of the North cannot hold out; it would have to be divided among the fortresses in order to raise their garrisons to sufficient strength.
    It is believed that the Prussians will divide their forces into two armies of 40,000 to 50,000 men in order to conduct the campaign more quickly. One will undertake

---
5 Armed with old-pattern rifles, and without noting 20,000 *Gardes Nationales Sédentaires*.

the conquest of the maritime fortresses,[6] Boulogne, Calais, Gravelines, Saint-Omer, Bergues and Dunkirk, the majority of whose inhabitants speak a Germanic dialect. The other will conquer the fortresses of the east, Arras, Douai, Lille, Cambrai, Valenciennes, etc., whose compact group will help hold the enemy.

Employing their methods of warfare, the Prussians will bombard the towns, whose inhabitants will undoubtedly wish to surrender after five or six days of shelling, which will have burned the majority of the houses. The factories, which are the easiest seen because of their size and which contain machinery and workmen of the highest value, will be the first hit. In consequence, these eastern towns of the two departments do not seem to me to be capable of defending themselves for more than a month. The Prussians will move from one to the other over a flat country which is covered with railways and excellent roads.

The group of the maritime towns could hold out longer, probably six weeks, owing to inundations being made and because of their proximity to the sea, which we hold. If the population agrees to defend them to the last ditch, letting their houses be burned instead of surrendering after four days of shelling, the Prussians will be forced to undertake a regular siege once they have burned the houses. I believe that in this case, despite the power of their artillery, that a resistance can be probably doubled in time and that it will take them at least two months and a half to capture all of them. In this case, many of them will have to be sacrificed, but on the other hand they will not fail to requisition pitilessly so rich a country.

I am forced to report that I do not believe that my second belief (the defence of towns to the last ditch) is viable. If a commandant wanted to defend a town to the utmost, he would have to have on his side the regular troops, *Mobiles* and people who own nothing, and whose patriotism could easily be roused. However, against him he would have practically all of the inhabitants, the *Garde Nationale Sédentaire* and doubtless the *Mobilisés*.

If the war is to be continued, it perhaps would be well in order to reinforce the west and south of France, whose military resources I do not know, to take from the region of the North a dozen good veteran field batteries whose members are accustomed to halt the Prussians. Perhaps 6,000 to 8,000 men from the regular army could be also drawn from there, but the energy and duration of defence of the fortresses would be correspondingly reduced if they were deprived of these good forces. Lille, 5 January 1871.

The commanding general of the Army of the North,

L. Faidherbe.

Appendix Q
Order of the day to the 22nd Army Corps during the armistice

After the review of today, the commanding general orders Lieutenant General Lecointe to express to the men his entire satisfaction of the eminent services which they have rendered in the cause of the national defence during the two last months of campaigning. By their admirable energy they have maintained the honour of our arms in struggling valiantly in conditions of incredible material inferiority.

---

6   When the armistice was signed, General von Goeben was on the point of beginning operations against the north by an attack on Abbeville with at least 30,000 men.

In the sad circumstances in which the country finds itself, it is necessary for us to redouble our devotion to duty in order to be ready to face anything, whether against the enemy or for internal difficulties.

We have to safeguard the liberty and the national dignity. The country, whose wishes have been expressed by the majority of its voters, must be the master of its destiny. Citizens in arms have the duty to respect its wishes, and I count on the Army of the North to fulfill its duty.

Cambrai, 2 February 1871.
The commanding general of the Army of the North,
L. Faidherbe.
Order of the day on the disbanding of the *Gardes Mobiles*
Gardes Mobiles of the region of the North, you have been disbanded by the order of the government. I cannot let you depart without saying farewell to you. You have fulfilled from the first day to the last the hard duties which the defence of the country have imposed on you. You can return to your families with a heart full of the satisfaction which is given to the honest man who has fulfilled his duty. You will be honoured by your fellow citizens as a reward for all you have done and borne for six months. I have frequently complained about the sufferings you have had to undergo because of an insufficient organization, and I see in you the makings of an elite force, which a new organization of the army I hope will use.

As to those who have avoided their duty by unlawful means[7] and who have not awaited the punishment of the law, public opinion will render them justice. During their lives they will bear a stain which will not be wiped out for a long time.
I close by thanking the officers[8] for the zeal and devotion to duty they have shown in their positions, and thanks to whom the majority of the corps have made remarkable progress.
The commanding general of the Army of the North,

L. Faidherbe.

Appendix R
Extracts from a letter of M. Gambetta to M. Jules Favre about the inactivity of the Army of Paris
In order to support my claim, I insert here extracts from a letter of M. Gambetta to M. Jules Favre published in the newspapers:

Bordeaux, 16 January 1871.
(Personal and confidential)

My dear friend,....

---

[7] Several thousand *Mobilisés* and *Mobiles* fled to Belgium before or after being called up in order not to go to war.

[8] General Faidherbe took his orderly officers from young men of the region who volunteered: MM. Decroix, Bourdonnay du Clésio, d'Hespel, Desrousseaux, Crespel, Masquelez, Montaudon and Haubourdin. They gave the most important service during the entire campaign and most of them gave evidence of remarkable military qualities. M. Crespel suffered a contusion by the bursting of a shell at the battle of Pont-Noyelles.

You see approaching ever nearer a horrible catastrophe for France and the republic, and you resign yourself to it, complaining....

You have allowed yourself to be brought down by hunger. You have not seized the favourable times and occasions for a victorious sortie, and even with the purest intentions you will fall like those who fell at Metz and at Sedan.

Perhaps you will attempt at the last moment an honourable [capitulation] without helping the country.

These great efforts need to be opportune in order to be useful.

If you had sortied on 7 January, as your despatch of the 9th said, Chanzy would probably have won a victory instead of being defeated on the line of Le Mans.

If you sortie today, tomorrow or the day after tomorrow, taking advantage of the time when the Prussians have stripped their lines in order to send 200,000 men against Chanzy and 100,000 men against Bourbaki, you can still win …

Concerning your military situation, I will explain it as frankly as I can.

In the west, General Chanzy, who my despatch of 31 December told you was at Le Mans, took the offensive again which was ordered following the operations which began on 27 and 28 December and which are still going on, has been forced out of his positions and has been obliged to retire behind the Mayenne. He had to resist the attack of an army of more than 200,000 men, commanded by Prince Friedrich Carl and the Duke of Mecklenburg. Reinforcements coming from Paris overcame him, despite a heroic defence which was unfortunately mixed with cruel weaknesses.

I send you the series of his despatches from the commencement of his operations until today, and by them you can follow in detail the circumstances of this terrible struggle. In them you can admire the strength of character of this brave general. The principal reasons for his defeat are the lack of coordination of his action and one from Paris, the panic of the Breton *Mobilisés*, and last the inexperience of their commanding officers.

The peculiar characteristics of the armies which we have raised are a lack of solidity and tenacity. The men cannot bear above all a long series of actions over several weeks which are partly successful but which have not yet brought them a victory of such magnitude to encourage them for a long time. This explains why from the beginning of the war our several armies have need from time to time to remake and reconstitute themselves after a certain period of fighting.

The men have been too quickly trained and fitted out, which means that they can march only on a certain number of days and that they need to be remodelled thoroughly afterwards. However, these periods should not weaken or beat you down since they are in the nature of things. It is necessary to be resolute, to not let oneself be let down and to patiently take up again after each loss the task of reorganization and resistance to the end.

Just as we did after the first capture of Orléans, the defeats suffered in November by the Army of the West, at Nogent-le-Rotrou, when Le Mans was threatened for the first time; in the same fashion after Tours and the second evacuation of Orléans, after the defeat of the army of Cambriels at Burgonz.

In the same way we are today fitting out the second Army of the Loire behind the Mayenne. I leave tonight for Laval to begin this task at the request of General

Chanzy. It is necessary so that these such inexperienced and recently formed units will really acquire a military temperament.

It is equally necessary for another reason. After several actions which we won, each time we encountered the Prussians with inferior or equal strength, they succeeded in accumulating very superior numbers at the decisive point. These could not have appeared in the case of General Chanzy if Paris had made numerous attempts outside its walls and a sortie which had no hope of returning.

It is quite evident that the army in Paris cannot solely be a defensive force. It must form an army for exterior operations, a relieving army capable of taking the field and by this means increasing the number of forces operating against the enemy outside Paris. I believe that the provincial armies have a dual role: to converge on Paris in an offensive role, or to take away from the besiegers considerable forces at some distance from the capital, whose absence will diminish thereby the depth of the lines of investment. But in any case final success is possible only when Paris stirs from its persistent inactivity at an opportune time.

It is furthermore necessary to remember that during the long series of efforts made by our young troops, beside the risk run by the enemy in moving ever farther from his base of operations, each day will cost him many men, and even if he is triumphant his forces will be exhausted....

General Chanzy is eminently suitable for this war of unceasing actions, whose aim is to wear down the enemy. Rest assured that in several days we will have reestablished the second Army of the Loire, to which the 19th Corps has been directed, and which will form its left wing, at Flers.

The loss of the line of the Sarthe is certainly of importance. Nevertheless, the consequences of its loss must not be exaggerated, because once the army is reorganized, General Chanzy could force the enemy to give up this line by a vigorous movement on the enemy right in the direction of Alençon. This operation could be supported by the 25th Corps and the mobile column of General Clecet, which is posted from Tours to Calerzon. In the east our affairs are going much better.... The enterprise of General Bourbaki, whose importance you will recognize, has already produced significant results.

The attached table of the despatches concerning his movements and the successes already achieved will be a faithful guide to all phases of the operations. However, I must state that, as in the case of Chanzy, that operations began in the last days of December instead of when I told you. In reality, for nearly twenty days these two armies have been constantly fighting, with varying success, but both in your interest, since the defeat of one and the success of the other are at the lest useful to you in that they keep far from you the best of the troops encircling Paris.

Friedrich Carl commands the Prussian armies in the west, and he has been going at Chanzy fiercely for 20 days. Manteuffel is the commanding general who has brought against Bourbaki 100,000 men, most of whom have been taken from the lines of investment. Werder has been stripped of command, for the Prussians arrange matters well and relieve generals who are beaten of their commands. He has gone to join von der Thann and Steinmetz. And during these struggles, what has Paris done? Nothing. Its population has held stoically under the shells of the

Prussians, but a population under fire is expected to do this not only in France but throughout Europe.

Your despatches have left us no doubt that time is pressing for you, so what are you waiting for? Everyone around you pleads you to do something.

I have sent you my opinion, I have explained the situation, I have given you the general opinion, which is unanimous in a sense for an immediate effort. To keep longer for whatever reason to the pretext of such weakness would be an act worthy of condemnation by the country and republic; I will not associate myself with it, even indirectly. You have the necessary strength and the right to obey.

Use it. But you will understand that I have a duty to make known to France your despatches, which are so characteristic on the situation and the military leadership of the capital.

In consequence, if I have not received by the 23rd a despatch from you announcing that a sortie has been made without hope of returning, undertaken with all the means at your disposal, I will make known the truth to France.

Gambetta.

Appendix S
Losses of the 1st Prussian Army

Documents from Germany have informed us of the losses of certain units of the 1st German Army. The following figures have been taken from them and may be regarded as more or less correct:

The 7th East Prussian Infantry Regiment lost 400 men in the battle of Amiens. The 8th East Prussian Fusilier Regiment [no such unit] lost nearly 400 men at Amiens and Pont-Noyelles and 300 at Saint-Quentin. The 5th Rhenish Infantry Regiment [i.e., 65th Infantry Regiment] lost 435 men at Point-Noyelles and Saint-Quentin. The 33rd East Prussian Fusilier Regiment lost 700 men, of whom 200 fell at Pont-Noyelles, 300 at Bapaume and 150 at Saint-Quentin. The 2nd Rhenish Infantry Regiment [i.e., 28th Infantry Regiment] lost 450 men, 300 of whom at Bapaume. The 6th Rhenish Infantry Regiment [i.e., 66th Infantry Regiment] lost 400 men, of whom 150 at Amiens and 125 at Bapaume. The 8th Rhenish Infantry Regiment [i.e., 70th Infantry Regiment] lost 400 men, 300 of whom at Saint-Quentin. The Rhenish White Cuirassier Regiment [i.e., 8th Cuirassier Regiment] lost 50 men at Bapaume. The 3rd Rhenish Infantry Regiment [i.e., 29th Infantry Regiment] lost 425 men, of whom 300 at Saint-Quentin. The 5th East Prussian Infantry Regiment [i.e., 41st Infantry Regiment] lost 250 men at Saint-Quentin. The 7th Rhenish Infantry Regiment [i.e., 69th Infantry Regiment] lost 250 men, 175 of whom at Saint-Quentin. The Hohenzollern Fusilier Regiment [40th] lost 325 men, nearly 200 at Saint-Quentin. The 3rd Railway Section lost 150 men. The Rhenish Field Artillery Regiment [8th] lost more than 300 men, of whom 100 at Saint-Quentin. The East Prussian Field Artillery Regiment [1st] lost a hundred men at Amiens and sixty at Saint-Quentin. The 2nd Hanoverian Lancer Regiment [14th] lost 300 men, of whom 250 at the battle of Saint-Quentin, etc., etc.[9]

---

9   Translator's note: it should be remarked that in many cases these figures do not correspond with the losses as given in the German general staff history of the war. Most would appear to be too high, but such exaggeration is natural.

Appendix T
Order of battle of The Army of the North about mid-January 1871
Commander in chief: Lieutenant General Faidherbe
Second in command [*major-général*]: Lieutenant General Farre
Assistants [*major-généraux adjoints*]: Colonel Cosseron de Villenoisy of the engineers, Majors Lucas de Peslouan, Mélard
Commander of artillery: Lieutenant Colonel Charon
Commander of engineers: Colonel Milliroux
Chief of staff: Lieutenant Colonel de la Sauzaie
Chief intendant: Military Intendant Richard
Grand provost: Major de Courchamp des Sablons
Chief doctor: *Médécin-principal* Laveran
Chief paymaster: Courtiades

Troops attached to headquarters
Cavalry (Colonel Barbault de Lamotte): 11th Provisional Dragoons: Lieutenant Colonel Baussin (Barbault de Lamotte)[10]: four and a half squadrons

Provost (Major de Courchamp des Sablons): two provisional squadrons of police
Artillery reserve (Naval Lieutenant Giron): 1st mixed battery (12-pounders) – Naval Lieutenant Rolland (La Chapelle); 2nd mixed battery (12-pounders) – Naval Lieutenant Gaigneau d'Étiolles (Meusnier); 1st battery of *Mobiles* of Seine-Inférieure (4-pounders): Captain de Belleville (Dieudonné)[11]

Engineer reserve: 12th company *bis* of the 2nd Regiment (Captain Grimaud)[12]

Engineer park: Captain Grimaud

---

10 The names in parentheses are those of the previous holders of the positions. The ranks followed by (A) are ranks of an auxiliary nature. The composition of the cavalry of the Army of the North is very uncertain. According to extracts from the histories of the 7th and 11th Provisional Dragoons, reproduced by Grenest, pp.138 and 168, it appears that the *Dragons du Nord* were initially formed at two squadrons from at least the depot of the 4th Dragoons at Lille and of detachments from the 2nd, 5th and 12th Dragoons. Then they took the name of 4th Provisional Dragoons. Finally, the 11th Provisional Dragoons were formed at Lille on 1 January 1871, from at least two squadrons and an auxiliary troop (*hors-rang*) from the *Dragons du Nord* (7th Provisional, 400 men and 270 horses), and from 50 men and 50 horses from the 8th Dragoons. It was at four squadrons. In addition, a troop of 35 horses, Sub Lieutenant Varin, served as escort to the commander in chief.
11 Jules Richard in his *Annuaire de la guerre de 1870-1871*, part 3, pp.91 and 93, allots the 2nd mixed battery of the 15th Artillery Regiment to the general reserve and to 2nd Division of 22nd Corps at the same time, with two different captains. According to this author, the general reserve should also contain the 4th battery *bis* of the 15th Artillery Regiment [it was part of the 1st Division of 23rd Corps], 1st and 2nd batteries of 15th Artillery Regiment. No information has been found about the role played by these two last batteries. M. Richard gives the effective cavalry of the army as two squadrons of the 8th Dragoons, which is certainly incorrect.
12 Formed on 13 December at Lille from escaped prisoners. Fought on 19 January with 22nd Corps, Brigade Fœrster.

Free corps: reconnaissance battalion – Captain Jourdan (Major Bayle); Volunteer Sharpshooters of the Nord – Captain Delaporte;[13] *Zouaves éclaireurs du Nord* – Captain Trouvé; free company of the battalion of *Mobilisés* of Saint-Quentin – unknown commander

Total: six and a quarter squadrons, 18 guns, one company of engineers.

22nd Army Corps
Lieutenant General Lecointe (Faidherbe, Farre)
Chief of staff: Lieutenant Colonel of Infantry Aynès (detached to 1st Brigade of 1st Division); Captain of Engineers Farjon
Artillery commander: Major Pigouche
Engineer commander: Major Thouzelier
Sub-intendant: Puffeney
Provost: Captain Bollenot
Chief doctor: *Médécin-major* 1st class Jourdeuil
Paymaster: Fourcade

1st Infantry Division
Lieutenant General Derroja (Lecointe)
Chief of staff: Major Jarriez
Artillery commander: Captain Cornet
Engineer commander: Captain Sambuc
Sub-intendant: Bonnaventure
Provost: Captain Monnier
Paymaster: unknown

1st Brigade
Lieutenant Colonel Aynès (killed 19 January 1871)
2nd Provisional Chasseur Battalion (Major Boschis). 67th Provisional Infantry Regiment (1st and 2nd battalions of the depot of the 75th Line Infantry Regiment, 1st Battalion of the depot of the 65th Line Infantry Regiment) (Lieutenant Colonel Fradin de Linières {de Gislain}). 91st Provisional Regiment (5th, 6th, 7th battalions of the *Gardes Mobiles* of Pas-du-Calais) (Lieutenant-Colonel Fovel {captain in the 33rd Line Infantry Regiment}). Total seven battalions[14]

2nd Brigade
Colonel Pittié

13　The Bayle companies were constituted at the end of October of *Gardes Mobiles* of the Somme, the Marne and Gard, to six companies of 20 men with one officer each. On 28 November they numbered 117 men; on 20 December they were reorganized with 300 men; on 25 December they formed the reconnaissance battalion. The Volunteer Sharpshooters of the Nord had but 24 men on 10 January. The *Zouaves du Nord* were part of the Isnard mobile column.

14　2nd Provisional Chasseurs, formed 2 October at Douai at three companies of 200 men taken from the 1st, 2nd and 17th battalions; subsequently raised to five companies. 67th Provisional Infantry, initially created with the 1st Provisional Battalion of the 65th, the 1st of the 75th and the 1st of the 91st, was constituted on 20 December from two battalions of the 75th and one of the 65th, with 2,400 men, including staffs. After 19 January the 1st Provisional Battalion of the 33rd appears to have formed part of this regiment. The depot battalions were also termed provisional battalions or 4th and 5th battalions. There were but six infantry depots in the north of France and not seven, as has been said. The depot of the 64th was not stationed there.

17th Provisional Chasseurs (Major Moynier). 68th Provisional Infantry Regiment (1st and 2nd battalions of the depot of the 24th Line Infantry Regiment, 1st Battalion of the depot of the 33rd Line Infantry Regiment) (Lieutenant-Colonel Cottin {Pittié}, then Tramond). 46th Provisional Regiment (1st, 2nd, 3rd battalions of the *Gardes Mobiles* of the Nord) (Lieutenant Colonel J. de la Lalène-Laprade) {Martin, Folliot de Fierville}, then Lebel). Total six battalions[15]

Divisional troops

Artillery: 1st battery *bis* of 15th Artillery Regiment (4-pounders) (Captain Collignon {Ravaut}), 2nd battery *bis* of 15th Artillery Regiment (4-pounders) (Captain Bocquillon), 3rd battery *bis* of 12th Artillery Regiment (8-pounders) (Captain Lannes de Montebello, then Captain Robert). Total 18 cannon.

Engineers: 2nd Company of 2nd Engineer Regiment (Captain Sambuc {Allard}).

Total 13 battalions, 18 cannon, one company of engineers.

2nd Infantry Division

Major General Dufaure du Bessol (Paulze d'Ivoy)
Chief of staff: Major Zédé from 33rd Line Infantry Regiment
Artillery commander: Major Chaton
Engineer commander: Captain Cantagrel
Sub-intendant: Létang
Provost: Captain Martin (Gontier)
Paymaster: Delahaye

1st Brigade

Colonel Fœrster (lieutenant colonel of the staff), then Lieutenant Colonel de Brouard of the *Gardes Mobiles*

20th Provisional Chasseurs (Major Hecquet). 69th Provisional Infantry Regiment (1st and 2nd battalions of the depot of the 43rd Line Infantry Regiment, 3rd Provisional Battalion of the *infanterie de marine*) (Lieutenant Colonel Pasquet de la Broue {*infanterie de marine*} [Fœrster], then Perrier), 44th Provisional Infantry Regiment (2nd, 3rd and 3rd *bis* [or 5th] battalions of the *Gardes Mobiles* of the Gard) (Lieutenant Colonel Lemaire {Saignemorte}). Total seven battalions[16]

---

15   17th Provisional Chasseurs were raised on 15 November at five companies, taken from the depot of the 17th Battalion. 68th Provisional Infantry, organized from 15 to 23 November at three battalions {two from the 24th, one from the 33rd}, on 23 November the last at five companies with a strength of 773 men. On 10 December it was at 658 men and on 18 and 20 December received reinforcements of 25 and 30 men respectively. On 31 December it left 22nd Corps and went to Abbeville, then passed theoretically to the 2nd Brigade of the 1st Division of 23rd Corps. It does not seem to have taken part in the final part of the campaign. 46th *Mobiles*: 1st Battalion of Nord at 18 officers and 1,200 men on 27 October, at 12 officers and 720 men on 3 January and on 19 January at 12 officers and 450 men. 2nd Battalion of Nord at 11 officers and 570 men on 3 January and on the 19th at 14 officers and 640 men. 3rd Battalion of Nord at 15 officers and 725 men on 3 January and at 11 officers and 648 men on the 19th. The regiment was 42 officers and 2,200 men strong on 23 December.

16   20th Provisional Chasseurs, formed 10 November at Boulogne from elements of the 20th Battalion; reorganized after the battle of Amiens and returned 12 December; six companies. 69th Provisional Infantry, raised 11 December at two battalions (43rd), to which was joined on the 20th a battalion of the 2nd Regiment of *infanterie de marine*. 44th *Mobiles*, created 12 November at two battalions (2nd and 3rd of Gard). A 3rd *bis* or 5th battalion was raised at Lens from 3 to 11 December by splitting the first two battalions in half.

2nd Brigade
Lieutenant Colonel de Gislain
18th Provisional Chasseurs (Major Pichat {Jan, killed 26 November, Wasmer}). 72nd Provisional Infantry Regiment (1st and 2nd battalions of the depot of the 91st Line Infantry Regiment, 3rd Battalion of the depot of the 33rd Line Infantry Regiment) (Lieutenant Colonel Delpech {Aynès}). 101st Provisional Infantry Regiment (4th Battalion of the *Gardes Mobiles* of the Somme, 3rd of the Marne, mixed Somme-Marne battalion) (Lieutenant Colonel de Brouard [major of infantry]). Total six battalions.
Divisional troops
Artillery: 2nd battery *ter* of 15th Artillery Regiment (4-pounders) (Captain Marx {Benzou}), 3rd battery *bis* of 15th Artillery Regiment (4-pounders) (Captain Chastang), 3rd battery of 12th Artillery Regiment (12-pounders) (Captain Beauregard. Total 18 cannon.
Engineers: 1st depot company of the 3rd Engineer Regiment (Captain Cantagrel).
Total 13 battalions, 18 cannon, one company of engineers[17]
Total for 22nd Corps: 26 battalions, 36 cannon, two companies of engineers

23rd Army Corps
Lieutenant General Paulze d'Ivoy
Chief of staff: Lieutenant Colonel of Infantry Marchand
Assistant chief of staff: Major Benoit de Laumont
Artillery commander: Major Grandmottet
Engineer commander: Major Allard
Intendant: Joba (Lafosse)
Provost: Captain Bergeron
Chief doctor: *Médécin-Major* 1st class Pappleton
Interpreter: Farinaux

1st Infantry Division
Post Captain Payen (Rear Admiral Moulac)
Chief of staff: Lieutenant Colonel of Infantry Jacob
Artillery commander: Captain Ravaud (Grandmottet)
Engineer commander: Captain Mangin
Sub-intendant: Lafosse
Provost: Lieutenant Goutier
Paymaster: unknown
1st Brigade

---

17 18th Provisional Chasseurs, formed from five companies (2nd-6th) of the depot of the 1st Battalion, and increased to six companies of 175 men on 18 December (2nd-7th). 72nd Provisional Infantry, raised 20 December as Provisional Infantry Regiment of 2nd Brigade of 2nd Division of 22nd Corps and called 91st Provisional during the same time. Became 72nd Provisional on 12 February. The battalion of the 33rd, reduced to about 350 men on the evening of 23 December, subsequently went to 23rd Corps, with which it fought on 19 January. One of the battalions of the 91st was noted as being in Abbeville on 8 December. 101st *Mobiles*, raised 11 December at three battalions, the 3rd being formed from the 6th and 7th companies of the Somme and the 6th, 7th and 8th of the Marne. The 3rd battery of the 12th Regiment was initially part of the reserve of 13th Corps. The 12th Company *bis* of the 2nd Engineer Regiment and not the 1st depot company of the 3rd Regiment appears to have been with 2nd Division of 22nd Corps on 19 January.

Lieutenant Colonel (A) Michelet (Post Captain Payen)
19th Provisional Chasseurs (Major Wasmer, killed 18 January 1871 {Giovanninelli, de Boisguyon}, then Giovanninelli after 18 January). Regiment of *fusiliers marins* (1st and 2nd battalions provided by the port of Brest, 3rd Battalion by the port of Toulon) (Lieutenant Commander Granger {Sibour, de Lagrange, Post Captain Payen}. 48th Provisional Infantry Regiment (7th, 8th and 9th battalions of the *Gardes Mobiles* of the Nord) (Lieutenant Colonel Degoutin {captain in the 75th Line Infantry Regiment} [Duhamel]). Total seven battalions[18]

2nd Brigade
Lieutenant Commander de Lagrange
24th Provisional *Chasseurs* (Major de Négrier, wounded 19 January, then Captain Joxe). Provisional Infantry Regiment (1st Battalion of the depot of the 33rd Line Infantry Regiment, 2nd Battalion of the depot of the 65th Line Infantry Regiment; 5th Battalion of the *Mobilisés* of Pas-de-Calais) (Major Rameaux {Lieutenant Colonel Jacob}). 47th Provisional Infantry Regiment (4th, 5th, 6th battalions of the *Gardes Mobiles* of the Nord) (Lieutenant Colonel Lebel {captain in the 69th Line Infantry Regiment} [Galliez, de Lagrange]). Total seven battalions[19]

Divisional troops
Artillery: 3rd battery *ter* of 15th Artillery Regiment (4-pounders) (Captain Halphen), 1st battery of the *Gardes Mobiles* of the Pas-de-Calais (4-pounders) (Captain Belvalette {Dupuich}), 4th battery *bis* of 15th Artillery Regiment (12-pounders) (Captain Dieudonné {Monier})[20]. Total 18 cannon[21]
Engineers: 2nd depot company of the 3rd Engineer Regiment (Captain Mangin)[22]

2nd Infantry Division
Lieutenant General (A) Robin (former captain of *infanterie de marine*)
Chief of staff: Colonel (A) Astré (Jeanne, dismissed)
Artillery commander: Major de Saint-Wulfranc
Engineer commander: unknown
Sub-intendant: Bohy
Provost: Captain Tailhade
Paymaster: de Bony

1st Brigade
Colonel of *mobilisés* Brusley

---

18   19th Provisional Chasseurs, formed in November from elements of the 2nd Battalion at five companies of 150 to 175 men; reconstituted at Douai on 13 December at five companies with about 150 men each; reduced to 400 men the night of 2 January.
19   24th Provisional Chasseurs, formed 21 December at Arras from detachments of the 2nd, 6th and 20th battalions, with a strength of 848 men; reduced to 645 on 19 January. Provisional Infantry Regiment of the 2nd Brigade of the 1st Division of 23rd Corps, formed 31 December from the 1st Provisional Battalion of the 33rd (which came from the 68th Provisional), a battalion from the 65th and a battalion of *mobilisés*.
20   M. Jules Richard, pp.90 and 95, assigns this battery to the headquarters and 1st Division of 23rd Corps.
21   1st battery of the *Gardes Mobiles* of the Pas-de-Calais, formed at Saint-Omer from *Mobiles* and several drivers and corporals of the artillery transport. Rejoined the army on 17 November. On 2 January received an officer, three non-commissioned officers and ten men from the artillery transport.
22   M. Richard places this company with the headquarters and also with the 1st Division of 23rd Corps, stating in turn that it belonged to the 2nd, then the 3rd, Regiment.

1st Battalion of Voltigeurs of the *Mobilisés* of the Nord (Major Foutrein). 1st Provisional Regiment (1st, 2nd and 3rd battalions of the 1st Legion of Nord) (Lieutenant Colonel Loy) (former sergeant major). 2nd Provisional Regiment (1st, 2nd and 3rd battalions of the 2nd Legion) (Lieutenant Colonel Dubois de Courval (retired lieutenant) (Dubreuil from 15 to 19 December). Total seven battalions[23]

2nd Brigade
Colonel of *mobilisés* Amos
2nd Battalion of Voltigeurs (4th of the 5th Legion) (Major Lacourte-Dumont). 3rd Battalion of Voltigeurs (4th of the 1st Legion) (Major Monnier) (from 15 January only). 3rd Provisional Regiment (1st, 3rd and 5th battalions of the 3rd Legion) (Lieutenant Colonel Chas). 4th Provisional Regiment (5th, 6th and 7th battalions of the 9th Legion) (Lieutenant Colonel Brabant). Total eight battalions[24]

Divisional troops
Artillery: 2nd battery of the *Gardes Mobiles* of Seine-Inférieure (4-pounder mountain) (Captain Montaigut), 4th battery of the *Gardes Mobiles* of Seine-Inférieure (4-pounder mountain) (Captain de Launoy), 1st battery of the *Gardes Mobiles* of Finistère (4-pounder mountain) (Captain Benoit). Total 18 cannon[25]

Cavalry: a half squadron of *eclaireurs mobilisés du Nord* (Captain Leclaire).
Total: 15 battalions, 18 cannon, one half squadron.
Total for 23rd Corps: 29 battalions, 36 cannon, one company of engineers, one half squadron.

Isnard Brigade
(also termed Cambrai Mobile Column)
(attached on 15 January to 22nd Corps)
Lieutenant Colonel Isnard (Martin, de la Saussaye)
Aide-de-camp: unknown
3rd Battalion of the depot of the 24th Line Infantry Regiment (Major Morlet). 73rd Provisional Infantry Regiment (depot battalions of the 3rd and 40th Line Infantry Regiments) (Lieutenant Colonel Castaigne). Provisional Regiment (1st and 2nd *bis* battalions of the *Gardes Mobiles* of Ardennes (Lieutenant Colonel Giovanninelli) (captain of infantry). 4th Battalion of the 7th Legion of the *Mobilisés* of Nord (from 11 January) (Major Plaideau (former sergeant major), at 750 men on 28 December.
Artillery: two smoothbore howitzers from the 15th Artillery Regiment, eight 4-pounder mountain guns (Lieutenant Wisshoff).
Total: seven battalions, 10 cannon[26]

---

23 1st Voltigeurs of Nord, constituted at four companies at the end of November. 1st Provisional left Lille on 16 December at about 1,630 men.

24 2nd Voltigeurs formed at a strength of 727 men and disbanded 2 February. 3rd Provisional left Lille on 16 December at a strength of 75 officers and 1,723 men. The commanders of the 2nd and 3rd Voltigeurs were former non-commissioned officers; those of the 3rd and 4th Provisional had never seen service. From 10 February the 3rd Voltigeurs was renamed the 2nd.

25 From 1 March 1871 the two batteries of Seine-Inférieure were converted into regular 4-pounder batteries, and the 2nd was attached to the reserve of 22nd Corps. The battery from Finistère, armed with rifled 8-pounders, also belonged to this reserve.

26 A 2nd Battalion from Ardennes had already been taken prisoner at Sedan. The 73rd Provisional was formed from 9 January by the reuniting of the depot battalions of the 3rd and 40th Line Infantry Regiments and split into three battalions. It had about 1,500 men on 19 January but was reduced to

Brigade of *Mobilisés* of Pas-de-Calais
Colonel (A) Pauly (former captain of engineers)
Aide-de-camp: unknown
1st Battalion of *chasseurs mobilisés* (1st of the Legion of Arras) (Major Garreau). 1st Provisional Regiment (1st, 2nd and 3rd battalions of the Legion of Béthune) (Lieutenant Colonel Poupard). 2nd Provisional Regiment (4th and 5th battalions of the Legion of Béthune, 5th Battalion of the Legion of Arras) (Lieutenant Colonel Choquet)[27]
Artillery: one battery of *mobilisés* of Pas-de-Calais (four 6-pounder Armstrong cannon) (Captain ----) [28]
Total: six battalions, four cannon[29]

---

700 men several days later. The Ardennes regiment received its packs only on 19 January. According to M. A. Martinien, *Corps auxiliaires créés pendant la guerre de 1870-1871*, Part 1, *Garde Nationale Mobile*, p.28, the Isnard Mobile Column had in addition the 100th Provisional Regiment (the former 48th *bis*) (10th, 11th and 12th battalions of the *Gardes Mobiles* of Nord), the 103rd Provisional Regiment (the former 91st *bis*) (4th and 5th battalions of Aisne, formed in three battalions). However, these formations do not seem to have taken part in the battle of 19 January.

27 This last unit, which had been incorporated into the 1st Division of 23rd Corps, rejoined after 19 January.
28 Did not take part in the battle of 19 January.
29 The Pauly Brigade had only 309 *chassepots* and percussion rifles. According to M. A. Martineau, on 19 January the Pauly Brigade also included the 102nd Provisional Regiment (Nord): 2nd and 3rd companies of the 3rd Battalion, 3rd and 7th of the 8th Battalion, 3rd and 4th of the 1st Battalion, 3rd and 7th of the 7th Battalion, 1st, 2nd and 7th of the 2nd Battalion, 6th and 7th of the 6th Battalion, and 5th of the 9th Battalion. No documentation has been found which confirms this statement.

Related titles published by Helion & Company

The Franco-Prussian War 1870–71 Volume 1: The Campaign of Sedan. Helmuth von Moltke and the Overthrow of the Second Empire
Quintin Barry
356pp Paperback
ISBN 978-1-906033-45-3

The Franco-Prussian War 1870–71 Volume 2: After Sedan. Helmuth Von Moltke and the Defeat of the Government of National Defence
Quintin Barry
536pp Paperback
ISBN 978-1-906033-46-0

A selection of forthcoming titles

The Science of War. A Collection of Essays and Lectures 1892–1903 by the late Colonel G. F. R. Henderson, C.B.
Capt Neill Malcolm, D.S.O. (ed.)   ISBN 978-1-906033-60-6

The Campaign in Alsace 1870
J.P. Du Cane   ISBN 978-1-874622-34-5

On the Prussian Infantry 1869
Capt Theodor May   ISBN 978-1-906033-59-0

HELION & COMPANY
26 Willow Road, Solihull, West Midlands B91 1UE, England
Telephone 0121 705 3393   Fax 0121 711 4075
Website: http://www.helion.co.uk